# Make Your Own
# ADULT VIDEO

MAKE YOUR OWN ADULT VIDEO. Copyright © 2006 by Quid Publishing.

First published in the UK in 2007 by

Collins, an imprint of
HarperCollins Publishers
77-85 Fulham Palace Road
London
W6 8JB

www.collins.co.uk

ISBN-10: 0-00-724853-9
ISBN-13: 978-0-00-724853-7

Conceived, designed, and produced by Quid Publishing
Level 4, Sheridan House
114 Western Road
Hove BN3 1DD England
www.quidpublishing.com

Design: Luke Herriott / Studio Ink
Illustrations: Rob Brandt
Photography: Petra Joy

10  9  8  7  6  5  4  3  2  1

# PETRA JOY

### with David Bramwell

## Make Your Own

# ADULT
# VIDEO

### The Couple's Guide to
### Making Sensual Home Movies

## Collins
*An Imprint of* HarperCollins*Publishers*

# CONTENTS
## A Quick-Reference Guide

# INTRODUCTION
## Why Make Your Own Adult Video?

Have you watched an adult video and found that it doesn't do anything for you? Do you think you and your partner could do better than the stuff you find in stores or on the Internet? Well, the fact is, you could have a lot of fun trying to make your very own home-made adult video…

If you are hungry for fresh, juicy, sexy action, then this book is for you. It will inspire your creativity and your sex life, and if you share this learning experience with a partner it will hopefully bring you closer together. You will learn about each other's fantasies and become each other's subject of desire. What could be more fun than the thrill of being filmed having sex? And what could be a bigger turn-on than seeing yourself in action on the screen for the first time?

Even if you normally shy away from watching the X-rated stuff, why not make your own? You'll have a great time filming it, and the finished product might be more to your own taste. That's my philosophy. Commercial movies do nothing for me. Sex sells; intimacy, sensuality, and creativity don't. I want to watch something that stimulates the mind and feeds the soul, that is creative and kinky. And because I can't find it anywhere else, I make my own.

Hardly any big-name producers dare to venture past the clichés of a Viagra-fuelled meat market. These commercial videos are cheap to produce and therefore make a big profit. They are shot in an assembly-line style: everybody uses the same studios, actors, and scenarios, and a 90-minute movie can be finished off in one or two days. Female fantasies are hidden, and male fantasies pleased to the max, which could be one reason why so many women don't enjoy the average hardcore movie.

Men and women are both visual creatures. We enjoy watching sexual images, and get bored and alienated by an endless parade of brightly lit genitals. The imagery of mainstream adult videos has become so blatant that it is almost gynaecological. There is no mystery left. It is the mystery, the unknown, that makes images sexy to me, so I choose to add layers, rather than taking them away. I use natural lighting and shoot through materials that create textures; I work with props that express the fantasies of the individuals I film.

I want to inspire you to be creative, to cross boundaries and let yourself be surprised when you have sex and shoot your first video. I want you to open your mind to a sexual culture of creating rather than consuming, and to expressing your sexy uniqueness rather than copying what you see other people do on film over and over again. I want you to be inspired and – above all else – to enjoy yourself.

*Petra Joy*

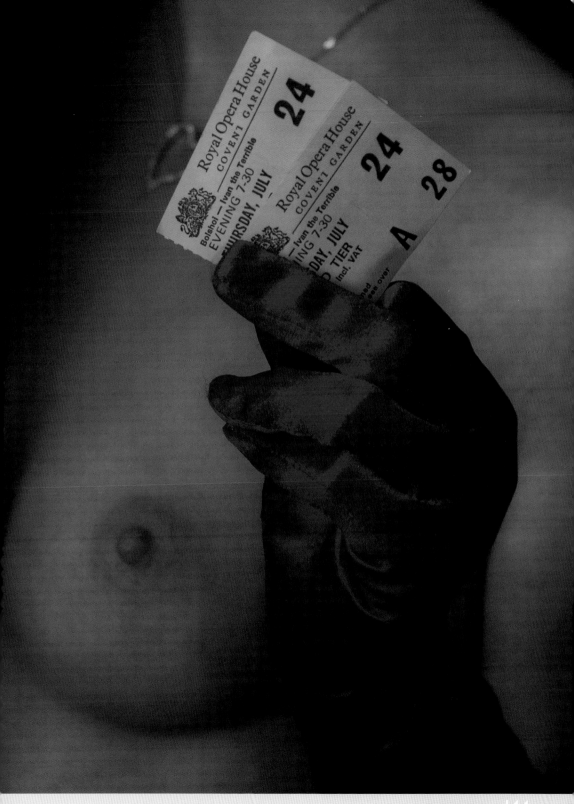

# ↻1 ▶▶ SETTING UP

By David Bramwell

# THE CAST
## Stars of Stage and Screen

Recording yourselves in the throws of passion is a lot of fun, but videoing each other having sex and making it look good is a difficult task to master – just ask Pam and Tommy. To handle it well, enjoy the process and create satisfying results, you need to be experienced in front the camera as well as behind it.

### Keeping it Real

One of the most fundamental decisions that must be made when making an erotic movie is selecting the cast and crew. Most couples decide – understandably – to do the whole thing by themselves, for themselves. Choosing to be the crew and stars of your own movie will, of course, give you a maximum amount of privacy. However, it also means that you will have a limited amount of technical control and fewer creative possibilities.

The reason is simple: when you are performing in front of the lens you have to learn to relax and forget about the camera, while at the same time being aware of it and being prepared to hold poses or repeat what you are doing. If, on the other hand, you are behind the camera, you will be able to concentrate on the technicalities: the framing, the focus and the exposure. If you shoot video you have to make sure that you get all the cutaways and connections

that are necessary for the editing; you have to monitor the sound (if you want to do it well, you need to do this with the headphones on), and set up and adjust the lighting. This is a completely different mindset to making love and letting go while being watched. Switching continuously between two mindsets in this way might make you stressed, and as a result you will not enjoy what you are doing.

### Setting Goals

It all depends on your focus. If your main aim is to have a sexy and stylish, professional-looking film of you and your partner being passionate, I would always advise getting somebody experienced to shoot and edit it for you. If your main aim is to spice up your sex life and you enjoy seeing each other naked or having sex, regardless of the technical quality, then the journey is the destination. You will simply enjoy the do-it-yourself aspect of erotic

photography and filmmaking, as long as you do not eventually get frustrated and give up because the technical quality of your images might be poor.

### Go it Alone or Get Help?

If you would like a record of the two of you together and are bored with unpredictable self-timer shots or tedious video rushes, you might want to look into getting a third person to shoot the two of you. In my experience, it is a lot more relaxing for a straight couple if the person behind the camera is female. There are two reasons for this. First, men tend to have been brainwashed by glamour photography and porn, and (unless they are true professionals) may enforce porn scenarios on the couple they are shooting, whether this suits them (especially the woman) or not. Second, men feel easily intimidated by having another man on set, whereas women often feel supported by another woman.

You might ask a trusted friend to video you as a couple. Or, if you have an open relationship, one of you might video your partner with another male or female lover – in which case, make sure beforehand that what you are going to shoot is something you have seen and experienced before, so that it will not make you feel jealous or guilty.

▶▶ **PRACTICAL TIP: STARTING OUT**

**To start your ventures, focus on photographing and filming each other. Learn how to direct each other gently and bring out what makes each of you unique and sexy. The challenge of making your first erotic movie is made even easier if one of you poses for the other. That way, one person can concentrate on 'performing', and the other on the technical aspects of shooting and directing the 'performer'. For one person to shoot and the other to model or perform is a good starting point – by taking turns in each role you will each learn the technical skills involved in handling the camera, and become comfortable in front of the lens.**

### Involving a Third Party

Whoever is behind the camera (no matter if they are a professional or just a friend of yours whom you trust), the person you choose should have the following qualities:

▶▶ They should know how to use the camera and have a basic understanding of lighting and sound recording.

▶▶ They should have a clear creative vision and be able to translate this into simple but effective directing.

▶▶ They should be able to direct without being too obtrusive.

▶▶ They should respect the boundaries you have set. If you don't want them involved in an on-screen capacity, make sure it's clear from the start. Personally, I always stay behind the camera and would never dream of getting involved sexually with a couple I am shooting.

▶▶ They should know that they are doing this film for you, visualising your chemistry, intimacy and fantasies rather than trying to impose their own. You have 'hired' them to make your film, not the other way round.

### The Next Level

If one of you has ambitions to be a 'porn director' and wants to have various people in the video, make sure you understand the following:

▶▶ You will have learnt the camera and its functions during practice shoots that cover aspects of your daily life. Don't waste people's time trying to find the button for the white balance while they are approaching orgasm.

▶▶ You will have discussed the project with your partner, including the involvement of the individuals taking part (whether in a technical capacity, or particularly if they are to be involved sexually). Make sure you respect your partner's boundaries. If he/she would kiss but not sleep with another person, don't try to make them.

▶▶ You will have practiced your directing skills. Never expect anybody to know what to do – you need to tell your performers in a firm but respectful way what you need them to do.

▶▶ You need to be sure about your creative vision rather than just asking people to 'get together and shoot something sexy'.

▶▶ Do not expect your partner or your friends to perform sexual skills or 'acting' on the level a professional porn star would.

▶▶ Cast everyone in roles they like and are comfortable with. When you come up with a scenario, see who would most like to be a certain character.

▶▶ Make sure you are well prepared for the shoot – have your camera cleaned and charged, and have a fully charged back-up battery, an extra memory card or tape stock, and a spare bulb for the tungsten light if you are using one. Know your location and try to have the kit set up before anyone gets there. It is equally important to get to know your performers. If at all possible, I like to spend time with people I will film before the shoot. It helps them trust me and relax during the shoot, and it makes me become aware of what I can and cannot expect from my 'performers', and appreciate them as real people.

▶▶ Do show you appreciation for your friends' help. This can be in the shape of gifts (you know what they may like: a nice bottle of champagne, luxurious underwear or simply flowers – the choice is yours but make sure you give

them something). Also make sure that you give people hard copies of whatever footage you have created and promised to share with them. Burn that CD with stills for them or copy the rushes or an edited version of the video footage. In the industry, models work for photographers in exchange for the stills. This is called TFP (Time For Prints, though in the modern age this is more usually a CD with the images on), and it allows both parties to extend their portfolio without being out of pocket. This barter deal only works if both parties honour their agreement. The same is true for you photographing and videoing your friends.

▶▶ Make sure that all the paperwork is in order before you even lift the camera. Your release forms or similar agreements need to be signed before the shoot.

▶▶ If you are an amateur and are looking for stars for your sexy flick, do not try to attract models and performers by claiming to be a pro. Be honest about your level of skills, hopes and expectations. This way, no one gets disappointed and you are true equals – a good formula for sex and creative ventures alike.

# THE BUDGET
## Counting the Costs

Your biggest expense in creating high-quality erotic imagery will be the initial cost of buying your own equipment. But even if you already own a camera and tripod, filters, lenses, a basic sound kit, a computer and postproduction software, your expenses never really stop...

Experience will teach you that it is useful to have a back-up for pretty much everything; at least one spare battery for your camera, and a spare memory card for your stills camera are essential. As you get more experienced and creative you might want to invest in an external camera flash (for stills) or an external microphone and proper lighting kit for video.

I also regularly spend money on useful materials that I can either shoot through or use as backdrops, and of course on fantasy outfits and props.

**Props**

If you have an idea about which scenes you might want to shoot in the future and spot a suitable prop that is affordable, get it there and then. It costs the same amount to buy a secondhand top hat as it costs to hire one from a costume store for a one-off occasion, so if you have some storage available, getting props as you go along makes sense and saves money in the long run. Material can be expensive, so, once again, if you spot something useful, get it.

▶▶ Masks are simple, affordable props that allow you and your partner to slip into different characters. They also guarantee your anonymity if you would like to publish your erotic photographs or film. There is a huge choice of masks available: they could be made of feathers, leather, metal and many other materials. For a range of options, try costume stores or the Internet. I love working with ornate Venetian carnival masks, which instantly transform a face and give the wearer a mysterious identity.

▶▶| **PRACTICAL TIP: ALCOHOL**

Use alcohol sparingly. Heavy drinking during a shoot is a bad idea – it will undermine your performance both behind and in front of the camera. By all means have couple of beers or a glass of wine to get in the mood, but, otherwise, save it for a celebratory drink once you have shouted "It's a wrap!" and can chill out.

▶▶ For a softer, more feminine look, feather masks work especially well. It can be truly liberating to wear a mask and nothing else, and it might bring out a completely different (sensual) side in you and your partner. I recommend Stanley Kubrick's *Eyes Wide Shut* for inspiration on the erotic power of masks.

▶▶ For each shoot there will be some props that you get in especially to create a unique style and/or mood. It feels good to surround yourself with small treats for your erotic shoot. Think about things that will look and feel good and indulgent: satin sheets pamper the senses, a luxurious bath lotion will help you to relax, and candles will give a beautiful warm light and create a romantic atmosphere. I also love using fresh flowers – they add a splash of colour, and their smell will titillate your senses during the shoot. Rose petals sprinkled on sheets or in a bath cost next to nothing, but look and feel great.

**Postproduction**

How much money you spend on your project after the shoot depends on what you intend to do with your images. If they are stills, are you planning to exhibit them? If so, you need to invest in the prints, frames and often also advertising or merchandise (such as flyers or postcards). If the video is for release rather than just 'for your eyes only', you need to think about the following aspects of the post-production: editing, cover and label design and printing, DVD authoring, duplication and advertising. You should also consider the licensing fees for any music used in the video that is not copyright-free, and the video licensing that rates your film as an 'adults-only' production.

Unless you are a multi-skilled filmmaker, photographer and computer programmer, and know how to edit, design covers and create DVD authoring that allows viewers to navigate the film, you will need to find professionals to do these jobs for you. How much you pay them depends on their

level of experience, how long your film is, and how time-consuming their input will be.

You might decide to burn DVDs on your home computer, which would save duplication costs. You could even print your own covers at home, but once you reach a certain level of quantity this gets so time-consuming that it is no longer economical to do it yourself. My advice would be that if you need more than 150 copies, it is definitely worth getting the DVD and cover professionally duplicated.

Such considerations are, of course, well beyond the means and aims of most amateur filmmakers. If, however, this is an area that you feel you would like to explore, more information can be found in Going Commercial (see page 130).

One last piece of advice on economic budgeting: shooting quality videos and photographs can be physically and emotionally demanding, so don't just budget wisely regarding your financial means – also bear in mind your personal resources.

# PROPS
## The Toys of the Trade

Part of the pleasure and excitement in making an adult movie is the chance it offers you and your partner to act out your sexual fantasies. To do this properly you will need to give some thought to props – it could be the perfect excuse to use something that you've always dreamed about.

There are plenty of items that you can use from around the house – such as the bed, chairs, silk scarves and handcuffs (for bondage games) – as well as the more traditional sex toys; it's all down to how imaginative you want to be! So whether you plan to be a seductress, master, mistress, stranger, voyeur or even Klingon love god, the accessories you use for your film will be instrumental in setting the scene.

**Outfits and Clothing**

Clothing can of course play a big role in creating an erotic atmosphere, from sexy lingerie to rubber and leather costumes. Personal preference will inevitably play a big part in your choice of clothing, but there are some practical and technical considerations to bear in mind that may not be readily apparent. The following paragraphs take a look at the main options.

---

▶▶ **PRACTICAL TIP: LINGERIE**

**It is of course all down to personal preferences, and shopping for the right underwear together is the best way to work out what's right for you. Different styles of underwear include:**

| | |
|---|---|
| **Panties and bras** | These are available in a multitude of styles and alluring fabrics, ranging from lacy and cotton to satin and silk. Ones with nipple holes or snap crotches can be ideal for filming purposes. |
| **Camisoles and chemises** | While the camisole is usually combined with French knickers, the chemise, being slightly longer, can be worn like a short dress. It makes an ideal prop for filming purposes, as it is demure, revealing and easily removed… |
| **Body stockings** | These are usually available from erotic lingerie catalogues, and whether sheer or lacy show off a woman's contours in a sexy, revealing way. |
| **Robes** | A lacy or soft silk dressing gown/robe will look glamorous on any woman and can be easily and gracefully removed once the camera is rolling. |
| **Bustier/corset** | These combine well with stockings and suspenders, and really serve to emphasise the breasts. They are best removed before making love, however, as they can tend to get in the way. |

---

 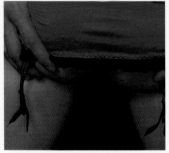 

▶▶ Lingerie:

From stockings and suspenders to lacy bras, camisoles and teddies, underwear and lingerie remain perennial favourites for turning a guy's head and making a woman look and feel like a temptress. Lacy garments have a very feminine appeal, while silks and satins are particularly alluring on film and sensual to the touch. For men, anything that shows off their butt and genitals is usually appealing, such as slim boxer shorts or tight briefs.

In choosing colours and designs, it is best to stick with simplicity – patterns on underwear and lingerie can sometimes be a little distracting on film, and while

Homer Simpson boxer shorts might be amusing, they are definitely not sexy. Opt instead for those tried-and-tested, provocative, sexy colours: red, black and white. Red and black symbolise power, mystery and mischievousness; white suggests innocence.

▶▶ Skirts:

Skirts are an obvious choice for showing off a sexy pair of legs, or for offering a revealing glimpse of a suspender belt. Skirt fabrics like leather and satin not only show off a butt but also have a vampish quality that really turns men on. Miniskirts or ones with long splits have the added advantage of being easily pulled up or removed.

▶▶ Tight pants:

If you've got the legs and butt for it, tight jeans or hot pants look sexy on any woman, but remember they cannot always be as easily removed as a skirt, once things start to hot up.

▶▶ Rubber:

Rubber clothing can look great on screen, particularly if worn under good lighting and polished properly beforehand. It is sexy, alluring and perfect for themes of dominance and submission. It can, however, be a struggle to remove – and it won't look good if your partner is struggling and going red in the face trying to take off a tight rubber dress or

## Talking Technical: Moiré

*One reason to avoid over-patterned clothing – other than on grounds of taste – is that it can lead to an unwanted optical effect known as 'moiré'. The scientific explanation for this is complex, and involves mysterious terms like 'lower harmonics', 'spatial frequency' and 'Nyquist frequency'.*

*Basically all you need to know is that if you wear, say, a shirt with black-and-white checks, it could well show up in your finished video as a bunch of annoying wavy lines. For the technically minded, the reason for this is that the subject has more detail than the resolution of the camera.*

T-shirt while on camera. This is something to bear in mind before you start filming. Rubber stockings and gloves, and attire such as short skirts, can, however, be kept on throughout 'play'. This might make them more appropriate items to choose if you're planning to leave the camera running while nature takes its course.

▶▶ Leather and latex:
Like rubber, leather and latex add a sense of sexual power, prowess and mystery, and their tightness and sheen can be very arousing. Good combinations include a short latex skirt and bra, leather bra and panties, long latex gloves and thigh-high boots, or a short leather/latex dress with stockings, suspenders and high heels.

For him, leather trousers and a tight T-shirt can look good, though it takes a special type of man to really pull it off and not look like someone's dad who's turned gay.

▶▶ Footwear:
It's all well and good wearing a killer outfit for your film, but don't spoil it all with tatty footwear. High heels remain a perennial favourite for making women look and feel sexy, while thigh-high or knee-high leather or latex boots will turn you from 'good girl' to temptress.

▶▶ Wigs:
Wigs are easy to purchase these days and come in various styles, sizes and colours, ranging from natural hues to bright reds, purples and even blues. They can be perfect for completing an outfit and will instantly change the way you or your partner look; ideal if you're planning to use your film to reveal your wild side.

## ▶▶ PRACTICAL TIP: UNIFORMS

**A great way to boost your confidence and enact your fantasies is to go the whole hog and wear a full uniform. They can be expensive to buy, but you could always opt for a hire store if you're only planning a one-off session. There are of course dozens to choose from, but some of the more popular options are:**

**For him:**
- Cowboy
- Dandy
- Builder
- Businessman
- Military uniform
- Tuxedo
- Doctor

**For her:**
- Fur coat (and no panties)
- Nurse
- Schoolmistress
- Dominatrix
- Business suit
- Princess
- Burlesque dancer

## Sex Toys

Sex toys make excellent props for adult movies, offering good visual stimulation, particularly if you like to see your partner pleasuring him- or herself. This is obviously something you need to be comfortable with, and so it is probably best to introduce it to your lovemaking prior to switching on the camera.

▶▶Vibrators and dildos:
Vibrators are widely available and come in a whole host of shapes, sizes and styles. When choosing a dildo or vibrator for filming, make sure you like the way it looks and feels, and that it's strong and well made – for quality, silicon rubber is still the best. Avoid novelty vibrators that come in the shape of a snowman or play a tune; they might seem funny at the time, but you'll soon get irritated hearing 'The Yellow Rose of Texas' every time it gets switched on...

▶▶Chinese balls:
When involved with anal play and stimulation it's always best to buy sex toys that are specifically designed for the purpose. Inappropriate and/or irresponsible behaviour is potentially dangerous – we've all heard the stories about people going to hospital with vegetables, chair legs and even

The more detail you put into your film, the closer you will be to creating your perfect fantasy scenario. Little touches can make a big difference, so why not consider using a few of the following to add that extra spice to your film?

- Satin sheets
- Soft lighting
- Feathers
- Flowers
- Velvet curtains
- A real log or coal fire
- Fur throws
- Candles

small pets stuck up their backsides. Chinese balls (also known as Ben-wa balls) can be inserted in the vagina or anus, and removing them can be visually stimulating.

▶▶ Massage oil:
Oils and lotions make an excellent all-round prop. They can enhance the romantic mood through their scent, and can deeply enhance the sensuality of touch. More importantly in this context, they add a beautiful sheen to the body, giving skin a luscious appearance on screen.

▶▶ Violet wands:
Violet wands have actually been around since the 1930s, when they were first sold as skin and muscle toners, and hair-restorers!

They simply plug into the wall and – when placed near the body – create an electricity transfer (in the form of a burst of small blue sparks) accompanied by a satisfying buzz and the feeling of 'being walked on by a kitten with its claws out'. They look very good on film as they are very colourful and erotic, and can be applied anywhere on the body. They should, however, be kept away from the head, eyes and all orifices because they are made of thin glass and can easily break. It is also best not to use a violet wand on someone with a heart condition or pacemaker – unless you're after their inheritance!

**Restraints and Blindfolds**

If you or your partner enjoy being tied up there are a whole variety of different props that can be used to varying effect. Applying restraints during filming can be visually exciting, but preparation is important – fiddling with complicated buckles, straps, padlocks or ropes can have the opposite of the desired effect if, after five minutes, you're still struggling to remember how to tie a reef knot. It can be worth setting them up before you start the filming, or at least practicing with them beforehand.

▶▶ Silk scarves:
Scarves are a simple solution if you want to tie your partner to the bed securely but comfortably, and are easier to undo than rope.

▶▶ Handcuffs:
Steel handcuffs look great and ensure rapid and secure application, but they can be extremely uncomfortable to wear. If used they must be handled with diligence; misuse or carelessness can cause damage to skin or nerves. Leather handcuffs are useful in that they can be separated and even worn from the onset of the filming. They are adjustable and more comfortable than steel handcuffs – some even come fur-lined.

▶▶ Bondage tape:
Bondage tape is easy to use, looks great, comes in different colours and is very versatile. You can use it to tie your partner to anything from a chair to her best friend.

▶▶ Blindfolds:
Taking away the sense of sight using a blindfold causes other senses to be magnified dramatically and can bring the feelings of anticipation to a fever pitch. With your lover tied up, you can film wherever and whatever you want. And watching the film together afterwards can be very erotic for them, as they see what was really happening for the first time!

**Whips, Canes and Spanking**

Most people don't mind a bit of spanking during sex; it stimulates the flesh, gives a feeling of exhilaration, is exciting to watch, and adds a rather satisfying soundtrack. For those who like to explore the pain/pleasure barriers further, whips, paddles and canes make excellent visual props and are ideal for visually reinforcing who's in charge.

▶▶ Bullwhips:
Bullwhips are highly versatile and make a satisfying crack. They vary according to the rigidity of their handle and length of the thong. (Shorter bullwhips are much easier to control in confined spaces.) Any bullwhip does, however, demand that the user knows what he/she is doing, or there is every chance that some serious harm can be unwittingly inflicted. Never crack a bullwhip towards your partner's face, and always make sure to protect your eyes when practicing.

▶▶ Paddles and floggers:
Paddles are short, portable devices; ideal if you want to film some over-the-knee fun. Floggers strike a wider area than whips, are easier to control, and are less prone to leaving red stripes on the skin. They are the perfect prop for teasing your lover's flesh, as they can be used to stroke the skin, while gentle circular swishing movements can be a more pleasurable sensation for those who want to be whipped but don't like the pain.

▶▶ Canes:
Canes are perfect for a naughty schoolboy or schoolgirl scenario, and can leave satisfying red stripes on a bare bottom. Be warned, however: they can seriously hurt!

**Food**
Films such as *Nine and a Half Weeks* have done much to make people realise how exciting it can be to turn sex into a culinary endeavour. Ice cream and whipped cream work especially well on film if smeared all over naked flesh, while chocolate can be heated and rubbed into the body. Why not turn your partner into a giant sexy dessert with whipped cream, ice cream and chocolate for you to devour in front of the camera?

# TRICKS OF THE TRADE
## Tips for a Polished Performance

When performing before the camera, you've got two options: you can play it real, or you can go for the Oscar. Both are fine – it's all a matter of what you're most comfortable with. If you do fancy playing up to the camera, here are a few tips from the pros.

### Sexual Positions

Though sex guides through the ages claim there to be anything from 101 to 1001 different sexual positions, the truth is more prosaic: there are essentially a few basic positions, but with almost endless variations. These basic positions can be determined by working out:

▶▶ Who is on top or in front, and which way are they facing?

▶▶ Which direction is the other person facing?

▶▶ Are either/both partners kneeling or sitting?

▶▶ Are either/both partners standing?

▶▶ Where are their legs?

▶▶ Where are their hands?

▶▶ Is any furniture/equipment being used (e.g. chair, hammock, sex toy, etc.)?

Certain sexual positions are favoured in adult movies – not for the benefit of best stimulation, but because they reveal more of the act of penetration to the camera. Three of the most popular are: Reverse Cowgirl, Fusion and Wheelbarrow.

For the Reverse Cowgirl, the man lies or sits underneath his partner, with his legs together. The woman sits on top (forming a 'T' shape), facing away from the man with her legs on either side of his. Endless variations can be created with the woman leaning back, forward, or changing where the man's hands are. If the woman leans forward as far as she can go, and holds his ankles for support, her partner (and camera!) get an up-close-and-personal view of the action and she gets G-spot-accessible intercourse.

For the Wheelbarrow, the woman lies on her back (on a bed or table), with her legs hanging over the side. The man, standing, straddles her and holds her thighs for support. For woman-in-charge scenarios, these positions can be reversed, with the woman straddling the man. Again, this is an ideal position for filming as the camera can get in close for a good view without disturbing the action.

The Fusion is a position where the woman will need to do more of the work – the bonus is that not only the camera but the

---

▶▶ **PRACTICAL TIP: THE MONEY SHOT**

In adult movies it's common to see the man pull out of the vagina before he orgasms and finish the job on her body, face or best friend. Known as the 'money shot', this kindly deed is strictly for the benefit of the male viewer, and it goes without saying that many women do not enjoy this in real life. As with anything in lovemaking, ensure that what you've got planned is something both parties will enjoy.

---

couple also get to watch what's going on. Basically, the man sits on the floor with his legs outstretched. He leans back and supports himself on his hands. The woman – assuming an active role – sits on his groin, passes her legs over him and supports herself on her hands.

### Porn Names

Whether you're a Ritzy Slickboots, Madame Whiplash, Tony Hotpants or Dr Bulge, inventing a suitably sleazy name for yourself and partner when creating your film can be more than just a bit of frivolous fun: it could help you lose yourself in your role as you prance around your bedroom, half naked, imagining yourself to be Captain Weenie and his faithful sidekick, Miss Behaviour. If stuck for a suitable name, try using the time-honoured method of combining the name of your first pet or favourite childhood toy with your mother's maiden name. Mine? Thumper Coulson.

### Keeping a Woody

Back in the old days, every good male porn star could call on the services of a 'fluffer' – someone to help provide the necessary stimulation to enable them to perform. In fact, the mark of virility for men in the adult movie industry then was not how many times they could perform, but how long they could keep a 'woody'. Since the advent of Viagra, however, all that has changed. Fluffers are now an endangered species and production time for adult films has halved now that the ladies no longer have to sit around for hours waiting for their male co-star to accomplish lift-off.

While the intimacy of making adult movies at home is less likely to warrant the services of Viagra, if you're trying to have a passionate moment while also considering lighting, continuity, etc., it's all too easy for the mind to wander from the task at hand. Need I say more?

### Facial Expressions

This may not be the first thing you think about during a blue movie – after all, the camera's focus tends to be a bit 'lower down'. However, your face is bound to be seen from time to time, and when it is it will more than likely be close up. At that distance, unconvincing facial expressions and uncertain glances will be picked up and magnified tenfold. The best solution is to try having a few stock expressions on hand. Those shown here are a good starting point, and can easily be practiced in advance using a mirror so that you know what you look like.

> ▶▶ **PRACTICAL TIP: DISTRACTIONS**
>
> I know it sounds obvious, but ensure all pets are kept locked up and out of the way when filming. It's all too easy to forget about them, particularly cats, who have an annoying habit of entering the room when you're about to do anything private in order to demand food, attention, thirty dollars and the keys to the car. The same applies to children.

### Cheeky

Not to be over done this one, as it can get to look a bit cheesy. Used sparingly, however, it injects naughtiness and an element of carefree humour.

### Ecstasy

An essential, this one. Of course, in an ideal world you'd be having such a good time that acting simply wouldn't be necessary. But we all get stage fright, so if you must fake it, learn to do so convincingly.

### Happy

OK, so this might not be the first expression that springs to mind during a hot and heavy filming session, but this is supposed to be fun, isn't it? It's always good to look like you're enjoying yourself.

### Serious

The movie will benefit hugely if you try to mix it up and play a few different 'roles'. The mean and moody look says, 'I mean business' and is excellent if you want to start dominating your co-star.

### Flirty

Try to flirt with the camera. A quick glance over the shoulder at a suitable moment is ideal and takes minimal acting skills. The key is to look right into the lens.

### Shy

You might not feel all that shy (and if you're naked in front of a video camera, there's a good chance that you aren't), but, again, this is all about adopting and expressing different roles.

# 2 ▶▶ WHAT'S YOUR STYLE?

By David Bramwell

# THEMES AND GENRES
## Choosing Your Look

At first, adult movies were more 'slot' than plot – most tended to jump straight to the sex without any pretence of a story. Curiously, the earliest surviving example, *El Sartorio* (1907), features three ladies frolicking in a river, when a man dressed as the devil appears and deflowers them.

### Stag Films

By the 1920s, the mass production of adult movies had begun in earnest, heralding the emergence of the 'Stag'. Stag films were strictly 'men only', and took their name from their regular appearance at stag parties. Stag films specialised in 'meat shots' (close-ups of penetration), rather than 'money shots' (men ejaculating on women). It wasn't uncommon in these films to see the male performers wearing masks to disguise their identity. More bizarre, however, was their insistence on keeping their socks on. Either through a mass bunion epidemic or simply because their families were such inbreds that they'd been born with 14 toes, these men didn't seem able to 'perform' without sporting a nice pair of cotton socks, making the masked man in stocking feet a classic symbol of the stag film.

America and France took the lead in production of these films, hence the term 'French film' becoming synonymous with adult movies, and it was the French who developed many of the genre's basic plots, as follows:

▸▸ A woman at home becomes aroused by a phallic object of some sort (it could be anything from a cucumber to a model of the Eiffel Tower). While masturbating, she is surprised by the arrival of a randy Frenchman, who is invited in... and the cucumber is out of a job.

▸▸ A doctor begins examining a woman and, true to form, asks her to go behind a screen and take off all of her clothes. Needless to say, several acts of severe gross misconduct ensue.

▸▸ A simple farm girl gets turned on watching animals copulating, runs into a farm labourer or travelling salesman, and sexual antics follow.

▸▸ A burglar disturbs a sleeping woman. Angry at having been woken from a sexual dream, she takes her revenge by tying him up and using him as a sex object.

▸▸ A furtive female skinny-dipper is caught in the act by a Peeping Tom, who then has his wicked way with her.

### Wall-to-Wall/Gonzo

Wall-to-Wall is a term used to describe adult movies that dispense with plot and, instead, consist of a series of different sex

---

▸▸ **PRACTICAL TIP: DRESS TO IMPRESS**

Costumes are one of the easiest ways to introduce a theme or imitate a genre, but you don't have to spend big. You could keep things basic and go for a seventies porn-star look. All you need is a large mustache and a nice pair of socks (both preferably sported by the guy only).

---

scenes strung together. Gonzo movies also rely on this format, and often purport to recruit amateur performers off the street (though in reality they don't, owing to the need for HIV testing).

In Gonzo porn the actors (usually the men) acknowledge the presence of a camera and talk to it, describing what they're doing, how they're feeling and so on. The female performers are sometimes treated in an unpleasant and perhaps even borderline-abusive manner, making this is an often controversial form of pornography that definitely will not appeal to every couple.

## The Movie Pastiche

In the last couple of decades, it has become almost *de rigueur* in the adult-movie world to ape popular Hollywood films. From *Shaving Ryan's Privates* and *The Bare Witch Project* to *Bridget Jones's Derriere* and *The Matrix: Deep-Throated*, if someone in the adult-movie world comes up with a good enough play on words, chances are the film will be made. (And if it wasn't for copyright, they wouldn't even need to change the titles of such classics as *Backdoor to Heaven*, *The Big Red One*, *Fist of Fury*, *Freddy Got Fingered* or *Up the Sandbox!*)

With few exceptions (*Flesh Gordon* is the only one that springs to mind), these films are awful: the acting's bad, the costumes cheap and the plot barely perceptible. As an idea for creating your own adult home movie, however, this can be a great starting point. Whether you want to re-enact a famous love scene (and take it somewhere the original never dared), play the role of hero and heroine in your favourite film, or just want an excuse for a spot of dressing up, a classic movie will provide you with plot, characters and action. For fun you could even mix and match characters from different films and different genres. You could have Dirty Harry and Calamity Jane, James Bond and Buffy the Vampire Slayer, or even Ben Hur with one of Charlie's Angels. If, however, you find yourself dressed as C3PO, about to make love to Digby the Biggest Dog in the World, it's probably time to seek psychiatric help.

## Drama

Many adult movies rely on drama as a means of creating different scenarios and stories with which to colour the action. Popular storylines seem to revolve around the world of espionage or crime, in which some young lady with ample bosoms and a willingness to please screws her way through half a dozen men in name of patriotism.

In many ways we have the seventies classic *Deep Throat* to thank for bringing plot (and humour) into the world of adult movie making. Still the world's largest-grossing adult film ever, *Deep Throat* tells the story of a sexually frustrated woman whose doctor discovers that her clitoris is located in her throat; hence she goes on to perform 'deep throat' on a multitude of men until she finds a suitable one to marry. *Deep Throat*'s use of humour, zany plot and a cool soundtrack paved the way for 'porn chic' when, for a short time in the seventies, adult movies approached acceptance into the mainstream movie industry, with other high-budget films such as *Behind the Green Door* and *The Devil in Miss Jones* attracting mass cinema crowds.

## Fetish

Essentially, S&M, Fetish or BDSM films all deal with the ritualised play of sexual dominance and submission. For those who take it seriously, the rituals, costumes and role-playing can even replace the act of penetration. Because of the sheer diversity and range of fetishes out there (from foot worshipping to cross-dressing) the market for specialised adult movies is ever-growing, and even if your particular fetish is for seeing chipmunks in drag being whipped by a transsexual Dutchman, chances are someone, somewhere will have made the very film for you.

S&M movies frequently involve the use of erotic garments to enhance the roles of the characters. A dominant woman (or 'dominatrix') will typically be dressed in leather, rubber or latex, carry a whip, crop or cane, and enjoy having her slave on a leash at her feet to satisfy her every desire. A dominant man may dress in a uniform or leather, and enjoy having his female slave on a lead, or tied up to be used and abused. *Fashionistas* remains a pinnacle of this genre of adult movies, having won countless awards for its lavish costumes, intelligent script and high-quality camerawork. Be warned, however: some scenes are not for the fainthearted!

---

**Famous adult movies:**

▶▶ *Behind the Green Door* (1972)
▶▶ *Debbie Does Dallas* (1978)
▶▶ *Deep Throat* (1972)
▶▶ *Emmanuelle* (1974)
▶▶ *Fashionistas* (2002)
▶▶ *Flesh Gordon* (1974)

▶▶ *Mona: The Virgin Nymph* (1970)
▶▶ *The Devil in Miss Jones* (1972)
▶▶ *The History of O* (1975)
▶▶ *The Marriage Manual* (1970)
▶▶ *The Opening of Misty Beethoven* (1976)

# SCRIPTS AND STORYLINES
## Porn with a Plot

The easiest way to plan a narrative is to write down your fantasies. Your story doesn't have to be an epic masterpiece – one page should be sufficient to convey your ideas. With your partner, discuss the setting, the kind of roles you'll be playing and the type of dialogue that would turn you on.

It is essential to keep your ideas simple for your initial film ventures. The golden rule is: the more involved the production, the longer the shoot. It's best, therefore, to stick to one or two locations (outdoors, in the bedroom, etc.) and keep the story brief. An erotic version of *Lord of the Rings* might look good on paper, but catering for 400 naked elves on the day could prove to be a real headache.

**Plotting a Story**

Good filmmakers always work from a storyboard (see pages 36–43). This is a series of drawings or photographs put together, rather like a cartoon strip, to illustrate how the story progresses. The dialogue for each scene is sometimes written below the relevant picture. Even if your film is not going to have a narrative as such, a storyboard is still essential for ensuring you

know what you intend to achieve with your film. It will also give you time to ponder on the details and practicalities of filming your ideas. If this sounds like a lot of hard work, don't worry. You don't need to be an expert illustrator – stick-men drawings can suffice – plus it's much easier in the long run to make changes at the planning stage rather than halfway through the filming. Here are a few ideas to get you started.

---

 **PRACTICAL TIP: PLANNING AND PREPARATION**

Here's a rundown of some things to consider when planning your movie:

- **What kind of theme do you want for your film: seduction, romantic tryst, voyeuristic encounter, kinky fantasy?**
- **Will you be playing yourselves or different characters?**
- **Where will it take place?**
- **What kind of clothes (if any) will you need for the shoot?**
- **How long will the finished movie be? (Don't be too adventurous: half an hour might not seem very long, but bear in mind that it can take two to three hours to make one good 10-minute scene, depending on what's involved.)**
- **If your story has a plot, what obstacles will your characters face and how will they overcome them?**
- **How will your characters interact sexually?**
- **Who's going to be handling the camera when the action takes place? Will you need a third party to film any of it, and, if so, do you both feel comfortable with this?**

Re-enacting scenes from your favourite feature films (with extra spice) is not as overambitious as it might sound. OK, I know I said that doing *Lord of the Rings* was a bad idea, but that's because it cost zillions of dollars to make, featured a cast of thousands and was filmed in New Zealand. Remember Demi Moore's phallic pot-making in *Ghost*, the elevator scene in *Fatal Attraction*, or the spanking incident over the boss's desk in *Secretary*? With a bit of humour and imagination, you can recreate moments from your favourite movies entirely to your own tastes and desires.

Literature, in the form of erotic magazines, storybooks and innumerable websites, has a wealth of stories and images that can help as catalysts to inspire and develop your own ideas. Men are well catered for in this department, and there is a growing body of pornographic literature written for and by women, giving greater knowledge of the kinds of fantasies that women like to act out.

**Dialogue**

What you choose to say to each other during your film is, of course, entirely up to you and your partner. Those of a theatrical nature may relish the idea of learning a script and playing different characters in front of the camera, while others may enjoy sexy conversations before or during lovemaking. Some strong-and-silent types may be more comfortable with no dialogue at all – that's fine too, and means that sound recording will be easy.

**Common fantasy scenarios:**

▶▶ *Doctor and nurse/patient*

▶▶ *Secretary and boss*

▶▶ *Teacher and student*

▶▶ *Innocent virgin (his or her first sexual encounter)*

▶▶ *Salesman and bored housewife*

▶▶ *Photographer and magazine model*

▶▶ *Prostitute and client*

▶▶ *Kidnapper and sex slave*

Anyone who's ever watched a typical adult movie all the way through will know that, with rare exceptions, the dialogue and acting can often be mind-numbingly corny. Vacant girls with cardboard expressions declaring 'Come on stallion, show me what you've got' or sweaty guys with beer guts shouting 'Drill me harder, you slut' can often be more of a turn-off than a turn-on.

Whatever your preferences, it's important to use dialogue that feels natural and that you both feel comfortable with. Below are a few different approaches to help you decide.

▶▶ No dialogue at all:

Not everyone talks or makes lots of noise during sex; some lovers simply enjoy being lost in the act of lovemaking, and feel no need or desire for all that moaning and chatter. If you would prefer to dispense with dialogue and other noises, remember that you can always create more atmosphere in your film by editing in a music soundtrack afterwards.

▶▶ Improv:

Improv is a theatrical term, short for improvisation, which in adult movies defines the use of unrehearsed lines and sounds for erotic effect. It is, of course, something we do naturally anyway when making love, and can range from moaning and giggling to simple lines such as 'Oh yes' or 'Do me harder'. Using improv is probably the best and easiest approach for allowing dialogue to come naturally and spontaneously in front of the camera. As a rule, women enjoy being told how beautiful they are, and lines such as 'I love your body', 'You really turn me on' or 'I love being inside you' will make them feel more desirable. Men will be flattered by this kind of dialogue too, but often enjoy more graphic phrases such as 'I need you to lick me' or 'I want you to suck my nipples hard'. If you do say something a bit corny, don't worry – in most cases it's only going to be you and your partner who see the finished product, not the whole world.

▶▶ Talking dirty:

A common fantasy for many men and women is to hear their partner talking dirty – telling them in graphic detail what they'd like to do, or have done to them, sexually. Part of the allure of graphic sexual language is that it is still a taboo in everyday speech, and to hear someone talking this way can be thrilling. Discuss with your partner what kind of things you'd like them to say to you, or you to them.

▶ Body worship:

Body worship – caressing, playing with and teasing each other's bodies – is in itself very erotic, but words relating to this play can have an equally arousing effect. Some couples even like to give their sexual organs nicknames, such as 'Tom's Turnip' or 'The Magic Cave'. If this seems a bit mushy (it is, but if that's your bag then no one need know), using expressions like 'You're so big I can hardly fit you in my mouth' or 'I love the way you taste' can't fail to get your partner turned on.

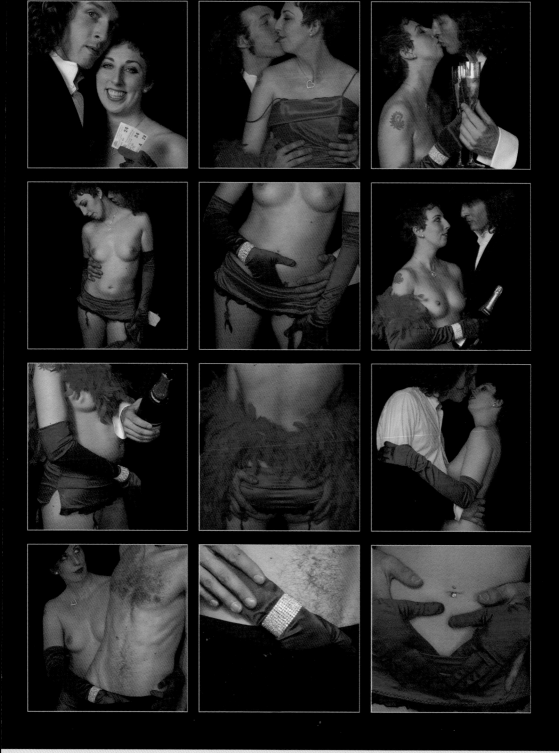

# CLASSIC PLOTS
## Pizza Delivery

Now to establish a basic plot. If this sounds excessive, think again. You might be full of ideas now, but once the camera starts rolling your mind can, and probably will, turn to slush. It's all too easy to fluff your lines or forget what's coming next, so why not sketch out some ideas first? If you're stuck for inspiration, try one of the classic plots illustrated in the following storyboard sequences…

*1. Start outside the apartment. The camera can stay in one place for now, so set it up on a tripod. It all begins when an unsuspecting pizza deliverer arrives with his goods…*

*2. The heroine comes to the door. Here is a chance to try out some of those expressions – serious, flirty, shy? This probably depends on who's taking control when the door closes. Best to keep your clothes on at this stage…*

*3. Take the action inside so that the seduction can begin. The camera could follow the heroine into the house, or remain static as the two of you enter the house.*

*4. A quick strip off and now we're really getting somewhere. She's in charge and he can't believe his luck.*

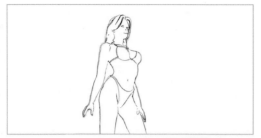

**5.** *Zoom in for a close-up of the heroine. Take your time! This will vary the pace of the movie and help mix things up a bit.*

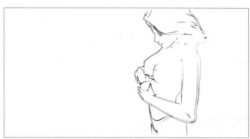

**6.** *She slowly undresses. Keep your distance with the camera to get all the action in.*

**7.** *Have the camera back on the tripod so you've got both hands free. Now the seduction starts in earnest, and could include some serious action as our hero is undressed and treated to some tongue work.*

**8.** *Experiment with some close-up shots; bring the camera near to her thighs, butt or face. These kinds of shots can be edited-in later and will contrast well with the more static long-distance shots.*

**9.** *OK, now it's all gone wild as she's got him over the sink, on the floor, against a door. But remember we want to see the action too, so why not try out a few of those 'professional' positions from Tricks of the Trade (see page 23)?*

### ALWAYS REMEMBER

**If you are planning to start your video outside the door to your house or apartment, it's best to keep your clothes on and save the 'action' for when you're safely inside. Neighbours have a tendency to pop up at unexpected moments, and you don't want to give old Mrs Johnson at number 13 a nasty surprise…**

# The Voyeur

For this one you'll need to find a good secluded spot by a river or lake. Failing that, the storyline can easily be adapted to an indoor scenario, using an empty bedroom and keyhole shots for that voyeuristic effect.

**1.** *Our heroine is bathing naked in the water. Her clothes are on the bank. Keep the camera static. Let it linger on her frolicking in the water.*

**2.** *Our hero is introduced, taking a stroll. The camera can be handheld or on a tripod, but should slowly track sideways to follow his movements.*

**3.** *Our heroine is standing up in the water now. Keep the camera relatively close and pan slowly down her body from head to toe, revealing her glistening skin.*

**4.** *Our hero has spotted her and sneaks over to a bush to get a better view. Again, the camera should follow him from a distance.*

**5.** *Time for a slow, lingering shot of our heroine from a distance. She is pleasuring herself and standing up in shallow water.*

**6.** *We see our hero crouched behind the bush. He is getting turned on by watching her and begins to play with himself. He makes a noise.*

**ALWAYS REMEMBER**

There shouldn't be too many problems as long as the video is for your own private enjoyment, but be careful when filming outdoors – in most places you can be arrested simply for being nude in public, let along having sex.

**7.** *There is a close-up of our heroine's face. She looks surprised, then it dawns on her what is happening. She beckons to the man to come and join her.*

**8.** *Our hero walks towards the water in his 'full glory'. He slowly undresses and goes to join her.*

**9.** *The two lovers meet, caress, and the fun begins! Leave the camera running on a tripod – any unnecessary footage can be cut out of this part later. From here on it's up to you as to where to take the story…*

# Women on Top

This is the classic erotic fantasy of the kinky female boss who likes to take charge! For those who want to spice up a film with sex toys and a little S&M, this is the ideal storyline, but remember to have your props set up beforehand.

*1. The boss is sat on her desk, facing the door, looking cool and imposing in high heels, silk blouse, tight skirt and stockings.*

*2. The door opens and in walks her secretary. His head is down. Oh dear, looks like he's forgotten to bring someone her morning coffee.*

*3. Return to the camera angle from the doorway. If you want to add a little dialogue, this is the ideal spot. With a wicked smile she orders him to undress.*

*4. Have the camera slowly pan down as the poor, harrowed minion undresses and begins to play.*

*5. Now she's getting turned on and lifts her skirt. You could go for a close-up here or use this point to reveal that she's holding a sex toy.*

*6. She decides to give him a little spanking and bends him over the desk. Set the camera on the tripod in the far corner of the room to get space in for this section.*

**7.** Have a close up of his ass after he has received his punishment. Those red marks should show up well!

**8.** It's all getting a little hot under the collar; she's decided to let her hair down, and strip to the sexy lingerie hidden beneath all that power dressing.

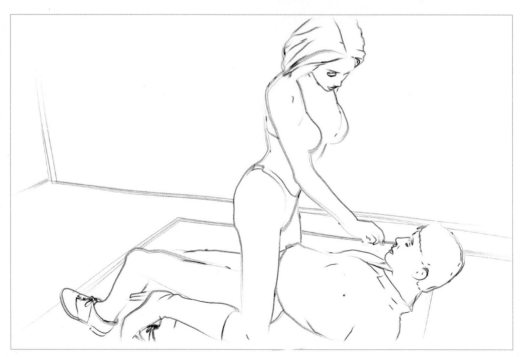

**9.** From here on in she's really going to use and abuse him. OK so it's sexual harassment in the workplace, but I think he's going to be too tied up to think about filing a lawsuit...

# The Romantic

You can set the scene for this one with candlelight, satin sheets, flowers, food, velvet backdrops – anything to add a romantic ambience to the proceedings. You could even go shopping for sexy underwear to get you in the mood.

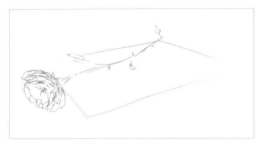

*1.* A rose and invitation are lying on a table. The camera zooms in to reveal the words: 'Your secret admirer', 'Hairy women drive me wild' – whatever floats your boat.

*2.* Our heroine is in her bedroom. She is dressed in slinky, silky underwear, and is looking through her wardrobe, trying to decide what to wear.

*3.* Mr Right is dressed in his boxer shorts in his bedroom. He too is choosing a sexy outfit. Again, ensure the whole body is framed.

*4.* The two are sat at the dinner table. Candlelight should give an excellent ambience. The camera should be on a tripod close enough to the table to box their upper torsos.

*5.* The camera pans back to reveal that Mr Right has slipped his hand under her dress.

*6.* Close-up of our heroine's face in rapture. Remember those acting tips and make sure you haven't got any of that bolognese sauce still on your face.

*7.* *Mr Right takes his lady by the hand; they stand up and leave for the bedroom. Keep the camera at a distance for this shot.*

*8.* *Let the camera slowly pan around to reveal our heroine lying on satin sheets dressed in sexy underwear. Savour the ambience and intimacy of this new location shot.*

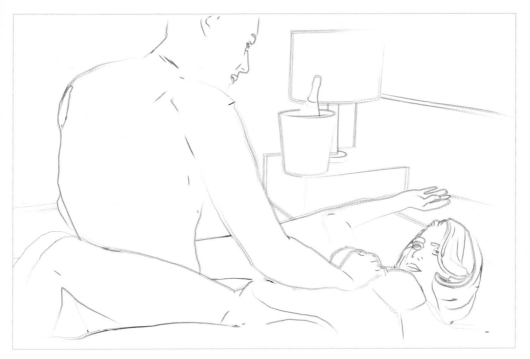

*9.* *Mr Right is naked. He comes and stands by the bed. He uncorks a bottle of champagne that is sitting in a bucket of ice. He pours two glasses, and then begins to tease our heroine with an ice-cube, dripping it onto her flesh. From here on you could indulge in chocolate play, massage, oral sex – whatever your heart desires. The night is young.*

3  ▶▶ VIDEOGRAPHY

# PRINCIPLES OF PHOTOGRAPHY
## How to Use Your Camera

To get more than just a few blurred shots of random body parts, you're going to need to learn a bit about photography. This section covers all you need to know. If you're thinking 'This isn't for me', that's fine, but try to have a play with your camera before you starting playing with each other…

No matter how sophisticated modern digital cameras might be, the basics of photography are the same now as they were were 150 years ago. Inside a lightproof box is a light-sensitive material, such as a film or a digital sensor. There is also a shutter, which can be opened for varying times to let light in and create an 'exposure'. A second mechanism gives you further control over exposure: the aperture. This is basically a hole, formed by an adjustable iris, through which light passes. In front of the shutter is a lens – this helps to focus the light pattern onto the light-sensitive object.

At this stage, the key thing to understand is that by altering some or all of these elements (shutter speed, aperture and lens), there is an almost infinite number of ways to shoot a subject.

**Lenses**
Regardless of whether you are using a video or stills camera, how an image looks starts with the type of lens being used. Most cameras have a single, built-in lens. This is fine, especially if it is an adjustable 'zoom' lens. However, you have more creative possibilities and choices when using more expensive cameras that allow you to change lenses. You could own a variety of lenses that will give you endless options for shooting images.

The human eye has a field of view that is equivalent to a 50mm lens, which is why a 50mm lens is often referred to as a 'standard lens'. However, other types of lens are available, and these produce different fields of view depending on their focal length.

▶▶ A zoom lens is effectively two or three lenses in one, as it has a variable focal length (e.g. 28–90mm or 35–105mm). By 'zooming' in or out, you will alter your field of view, and therefore how much of the subject you actually see: zoom out to see more of a scene; zoom in to fill the frame with your subject. This is the type of lens most commonly found on digital video camcorders and compact cameras.

▶▶ A wide-angle lens allows a bigger field of view, and is very useful in small spaces where you cannot physically step any further back from your subject. For example, say you would like to shoot your partner lying on a bed, but you can't fit their whole body into the frame when using a 50mm lens because the room is too small. Swap to a 28mm lens (which is a common focal length for a wide-angle), and you should be able to frame the picture the way you want to. There is a downside to using wide-angle lenses, though: they produce distortions when used close up. If you get too close to a person when shooting a facial portrait, for example, the images can look comical, with a huge nose and other distorted features. Unless this is an effect you deliberately

## Talking Technical: Digital Zoom

*If you have used a digital camera in the past, you might have been tempted to use the 'digital zoom' when your optical zoom (i.e. the zoom provided by your lens) doesn't get you close enough to the action. My advice is not to use the digital zoom. It isn't actually a 'real'* *zoom, but is in fact a function that simply crops and then magnifies an image. This results in very poor picture quality, which shows up as graininess on video and 'pixellation' in stills, and will prevent you from seeing all the interesting bits.*

---

want to achieve, it is therefore best not to use a wide-angle lens for close-up images.

 Telephoto lenses start at about 60mm and increase in focal length to 150mm for a short telephoto, and as much as 1200mm for a long telephoto (although this only refers to fixed lenses rather than zoom lenses, which rarely go higher than a maximum of 300mm). Picture a press photographer trying to get a topless shot of the latest celebrity, spying on her from a long way off. They would use a long telephoto lens of maybe 600mm or more. Lenses like this, with long focal lengths, allow you to make distant things look a lot closer – much like looking through powerful binoculars. Telephoto lenses also make the background look out of focus and blurred (or 'soft'), and thus emphasise the main subject, which is one of the reasons why they are ideal for taking striking portrait shots.

### Autofocus and Focus Lock

Virtually all modern cameras are equipped with an autofocus function that makes it easy to focus the lens correctly. However, there are some situations when you cannot rely on your camera's autofocus – it does not work well in low light conditions, for example.

At this point it becomes necessary to use manual focus. In such instances, always focus on the eyes (assuming you want them in the shot!). The eyes are the most important feature in a facial portrait, not the nose, which is on slightly different focus plane than the eyes.

---

### ▶▶ PRACTICAL TIP: LENS CARE

The quality of the lens is one really important factor in the quality of images you will be able to create with your camera. You may have used a disposable camera with a simple fixed lens. No wonder that most pictures never looked really sharp – the lens is just a hole covered by a tiny piece of plastic! Sometimes, a small digital camera that has a low resolution of only two megapixels (2MP) but a very high quality lens will produce sharper, better pictures than a camera with a better resolution but a cheap lens.

The lens is the eye of your camera. Make sure you do not damage it, because it will ruin your pictures. From a fingerprint to a scratch, whatever is on the lens will appear in your photos. When you change lenses or handle your camera, never actually touch the glass part of your lens with your fingers – use a special cleaning cloth or gloves. Lenses are usually coated with a special solution that stops internal reflections – greasy fingerprints on the lens can destroy this important coating. Lastly, always use the lens cap when transporting your camera to protect it from scratches.

Another potential failing of autofocus is that many versions focus automatically on whatever is exactly in the middle of the frame. If your intended subject is slightly off-centre (which he/she often will be), the autofocus will focus on whatever is in the centre of your viewfinder – even if it is a trash can! The best way round this is to use manual focus, but if your camera doesn't have that option, you can solve the problem by using a technique called 'focus lock'. You place the subject in the centre of the frame and press down slightly on the shutter button until the image is focused. Then, keeping the button semi-depressed, re-frame the image the way you want it to look, and then fire away. The autofocus will have locked onto your main subject, and the focus will be correct.

**These shots show how, by using manual focus and by controlling depth of field, it is possible to shift attention from one part of an image to another.**

**Exposure Controls**

Apart from being focused properly on its significant parts, it is important for an image to be 'exposed' correctly for it to work. Exposure refers to the amount of light that is recorded; an overexposed image will be too light, while an underexposed image will be too dark. Ultimately, if the exposure is completely wrong, no visible detail will remain and the image will be worthless. Exposure is controlled through two functions: shutter speed and aperture.

The aperture controls the size of the opening of the lens, and therefore how much light will fall on each frame. A smaller aperture lets in less light, a larger one more. Apertures are described by a sequence of 'stops' known as f-numbers (see opposite). Confusingly, the higher the f-number, the smaller the opening. Thus, f/16 is an almost closed aperture that lets in very little light.

**Underexposed image**

**Correctly exposed image**

**Overexposed image**

It is also worth noting at this stage that the aperture affects depth of field (i.e. the amount of an image that appears to be in sharp focus). A smaller opening of the iris (higher f-number) allows a greater depth of field, while a larger opening (lower f-number) will result in a reduced depth of field.

The shutter speed determines the amount of time for which each frame is exposed. Like aperture, it is described by a sequence of stops, but this time measured in seconds or fractions of a second: 1sec, 1/2sec, 1/4sec, 1/8sec, 1/15sec, 1/30sec, 1/60sec, 1/125sec, 1/250sec and so on. Many compact still cameras, and certainly all SLR cameras and up-market DV camcorders, allow you to adjust the shutter to expose either for a shorter or longer period of time. A decreased opening time, or fast shutter speed, captures only an instant of the action happening and therefore 'freezes' it – which is why it is frequently used in sports photography. A longer exposure, or slow shutter speed, captures more of the action. Motion is recorded as a blur; the longer the exposure, the more blurred it will be. This is something that you can use as a creative tool for photography and video alike.

**Setting Exposure Manually**

It is important to note that there is a direct correlation between shutter speed and aperture.

---

**Talking Technical: Aperture Sizes**

*This simple diagram demonstrates the relationship between aperture size and f-numbers.*

*Note: the higher the f-number, the smaller the opening created, and vice versa.*

*f/2.8*

*f/5.6*

*f/16*

A shorter shutter speed, for example, must be offset by an equivalent increase in the size of the aperture (a lower f-number) to achieve the same exposure. Most stills cameras will automatically adjust the aperture to the new shutter speed chosen. However, when you shoot video, the camera will not alter the aperture and you must close the iris down manually so that the sequence remains correctly exposed.

**Auto vs. Manual Exposure**

Most cameras have an AE (autoexposure) facility that will set what it perceives to be the correct combination of aperture and shutter speed. This will produce a good, accurate exposure in the majority of cases, but it can be useful to set the exposure manually in some conditions. For example, if a scene contains harshly contrasting patches of sunshine and shadow, the AE facility is unlikely to expose the image satisfyingly. The results would be unpredictable. One possibility is that the camera will try to brighten up the dark parts of the image. The problem with this is that the already-bright parts will become too bright and all of the detail in these areas will be lost. A better option is to take control and set the exposure

yourself. You might choose to reduce the exposure a stop or two so that the skin tones are nice and flattering, and the shadows truly deep and dark. Such a contrast can look dramatic and exciting.

**Exposure Compensation**

Even if you have a basic compact camera that lacks the functions to control aperture and shutter speed manually, you might still have 'AE compensation'. This allows you to increase or decrease exposure manually in one-stop or half-stop increments, and means that you can fine-tune the settings provided by your camera's AE system. This control also comes in handy if a subject is backlit (i.e. with a bright light like the sun behind it). Ordinarily, you can either shoot backlit subjects as a silhouette, or use flash to balance the overall lighting. With AE compensation you can make the subject lighter little by little until you like the look and feel of the image, rather than surrendering to the limited options the camera would suggest automatically.

**Slow Shutter Speeds**

I frequently use a slow shutter speed for erotic photographs, especially in combination with a flash – it produces images that are 'moody' and atmospheric, unlike

straightforward flash photography, which can be flat and uninspiring. Make sure the camera is well supported on a tripod, beanbag, or any flat surface you can find, so that camera shake will not ruin the picture. Slow shutter speeds also work well in combination with flash at night-time, when there might be other sources of light around like neon lights, candlelight or the flames of a fire. Combining a slow shutter speed with flash lighting in this way is called 'slow-sync flash'.

Slow shutter speeds look great on video, too. One of my chief requirements when choosing my professional and domestic digital video equipment is that it has this function. My DV camcorder allows me to switch between four different slow shutter speeds, each of which produces different degrees of motion blur. I have used this to great effect in my erotic films, and it adds an aura of mystery to certain scenarios. The motion suggests what is happening sexually, but because it is slowed down and slightly blurred, the details are left to the viewer's imagination.

I particularly like this effect because it looks very organic and not at all electronic, and it is not something that can be 'faked' later in postproduction.

## Talking Technical: Camera Shake

*Photographs can feature two types of image blur. The first, generally deliberate, type is that generated if your subject moves when the shutter is open. The second, generally unwanted, type is generated if the camera moves while the shutter is open; this is known as 'camera shake.' To avoid this and achieve a pin-sharp image like that below, you should use a fast shutter speed and/or support the camera using a tripod or beanbag. However, if you do not just accidentally wobble your camera, but instead move it consciously while using a slow shutter speed (perhaps by panning it along with the action), you can create some astonishing results. There are no hard-and-fast rules for which shutter speed might create exactly the effect you want, so you have experiment and be patient. If you find a shutter speed that works well in combination with the available light and flash, make a note of it and the other contributing factors for future reference.*

# COMPOSITION
## The Secret of Looking Good

**Have you ever wondered why it sometimes happens that photos taken with a cheap throw-away camera look great while those taken using expensive professional gear just don't look right? Well, as the saying goes, it's not what you use that counts, it's the way you use it.**

To shoot a video that works and looks impressive, you need more than just a top-of-the-range camera or the correct focus and exposure – you need an eye for good composition.

Some people simply have an eye for what looks good, some people don't. Don't worry if you haven't got it yet, you can learn a few simple rules of composition that will please the viewer. You will have to think before you shoot at first, but with time and practice the rules of composition will become second nature.

**Basic Considerations**

The most important thing is that you don't rush anything. Don't just point and shoot randomly – unless you're taking a spontaneous snapshot that cannot be set up deliberately. Think about what you see, then consciously choose how you can capture it. Move around and assume different positions – this will help you to visualise how your subject will look from varying angles. Choose the best option for the camera angle, position and settings so that you can really do justice to the person and/or scene you are about to shoot. The word 'video' comes from Latin and actually means 'I see'. So open your eyes, be aware of what you see, and then decide how you will get your vision across in an image. Here are some simple tips that will help beginners:

▸▸ Decide which lens to use. Are you going to shoot a close-up with a blurred background, or are you planning a wide-angle shot

that captures your subject in its wider environment? For the former, choose a telephoto lens and use a large aperture.

▸▸ Choose what angle you are shooting from. A common beginner's mistake is to work exclusively from eye level. I shoot a lot of full-body shots from a stepladder to get a bird's-eye view. This way, I get the whole body in shot, rather than just the upper or lower body. Sometimes you might want to adopt a lower viewpoint, looking up to your subject. Maybe your partner has dressed up for a dominant role – by looking up at them the images you create will enhance this fact.

▸▸ Think about how best to capture the essence of the shot. When shooting a dominatrix, you could shoot just her hands holding a whip handle. This mysterious close-up would send out a powerful message. Focusing on details produces more exciting results than a broader shot, because they are more unusual and thought-provoking.

▶▶ Be brave and fill the frame, maybe even cropping your subject slightly rather than leaving lots of room around the edges. Although you can crop digital images later on, it's good to get into the habit of framing correctly in-camera. Cropping will reduce the size of your images, because pixels are literally discarded during the process and this can affect image quality.

▶▶ Do not assume that your subject has always got to be dead centre in the image. It can look a lot more interesting if they are slightly off-centre. If they are looking or moving to one side, leave room on that side of the frame, so that they have somewhere to look at or move towards. That goes for stills photography as much as video, where you always have to pan slightly ahead of the action to avoid a 'caged-in' feeling.

## Talking Technical: Rule of Thirds

*A long-standing and easy-to-follow principle of composition is the 'rule of thirds'. Imagine an image that is divided into a grid of nine equal squares by two horizontal and two vertical lines. The theory goes that an image looks appealing if the important part of the picture is placed on one of these lines, or at a point where two of them meet. In facial portraits, for example, try to have the eyes of the model about one-third of the way down the frame and slightly to one side, rather than in the middle of the image.*

### Creating Depth

Images look more interesting if you incorporate different 'layers' in the shot to give more depth and create the illusion of three dimensions. For example, you could shoot your partner lazing on a towel with the swimming pool in the background and a plant in the foreground. This not only creates depth but also an exciting effect that suggests that you are watching someone secretly. Be careful, however, not to use autofocus with this technique, as it might focus on the plant or the pool rather than your partner, especially if he/she happens to be off-centre. One of my favourite techniques in erotic photography is to shoot through a semi-transparent material such as lace. The material layer creates and exciting keyhole effect (see page 117). It can also be effective to shoot through a doorway or window, thus creating a frame within a frame.

Be careful with cluttered backgrounds. If there is a plant or antenna behind your subject, it might look like it is growing out of their head. Optical illusions of this type are common in snapshots, where they don't really matter, but are best avoided in erotic images. Have a look at what is behind your model before you shoot; if there is something that might look odd, either move the camera or the object, or create a neutral background with a plain backdrop.

### Reviewing and Editing

When you shoot digitally, you can look back at the results of your work immediately. If the image does not look right, stop and ask yourself 'Why doesn't it work, and what can I change to make it succeed?' Give yourself plenty of time and change some factors until you find the image finally works. You can always delete the unwanted shots later.

Creating perfect images is a process. I find that I have to shoot about 20 images in order to get one real 'winner' where everything comes together and the overall composition is a complete success.

# CAMERAWORK
## A Crash Course

Shooting a beach scene on vacation or filming a friend's party is one thing; making your own private 'action' movie is a whole different ball game. If you want to produce a film that you can actually watch – whether it's one minute long or a whole hour – it helps if you learn to use the camera more effectively.

### Before You Start

There's a lot to think about when shooting your own adult movie, and if you're not careful your 'performance' will start to suffer as a result. Of course, you'll want to keep it fun and spontaneous, but working out a few things in advance will at least ensure that you look better on camera than Paris Hilton did.

Before you start shooting, you need to know your 'story': its beginning, climax and end.

Even if you have decided against acting or dialogue, and there is no script as such, you need to have an idea of what you are going to shoot and – most importantly – how you are going to shoot it.

It really helps to write down a shot list of must-have scenes and shots. You need to decide before the shoot how you want the scenes to look, and how you would like to fuse the sequences together later in postproduction. Rather than just getting your

girlfriend or boyfriend to strip for you spontaneously, you need to have a concept of how you are going to capture that special moment. This still allows room for improvisation for both of you, but makes sure that you do not end up with a pile of 'useless' rushes that are boring to watch because you pretty much shot everything in one take, without a choice of different shots, so the sequence cannot be edited properly.

 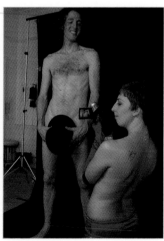 

Remember to 'go down' as often as possible... Experiment and be inventive with your camera angles – the world doesn't have to be seen from eye level.

## Size Matters

A key to successful editing is to remember to vary the size and angle of your shots within a sequence. This way, you will be able to edit this sequence without creating a boring montage of images that look the same. Size matters; therefore, aim to frame shots creatively. There is a huge variety of framing possibilities. It is a typical beginner's mistake not to vary the shot sizes, and to shoot too many mid-shots. The secret to creative camera work is not just to play it safe with average mid-shots, but also to dare to shoot extreme close-ups (lips being licked or an eye being shut) that make a sequence visually interesting and erotically exciting. Make sure you light these close-ups in the same way as the wider shots, otherwise you will ruin the visual continuity and have problems in the edit suite.

Don't be afraid of using extreme camera angles. If you shoot your whole video at eye level, it might  become repetitive. Shooting from a bird's-eye view is a useful angle to put things into a bigger context. The opposite angle – looking up from ground level – can be used to make people look impressive or superior.

### Point-of-View Shots

Point-of-view shots are an exciting way of showing the viewer what your main characters are seeing. If you shoot each other during sex, swap the camera round and point it at your partner.

---

### ▶▶| PRACTICAL TIP: KEEP IT CLEAN

**Sex can be a messy business, so check the lens for dust and other 'marks' during filming; when necessary, wipe it clean with a specially manufactured cloth. Even if you cannot see dust specks or fingerprints that are on the lens in the viewfinder or on the LCD screen, it is very likely that they are there, and they could ruin some beautiful shots.**

You will need a wide-angle lens when you are up close and personal, with the camera right on top of your partner – without it you would be too close to shoot anything but close-ups. By shooting each other in this way and sharing your points of view (or 'POVs') you will see yourself and your body from new angles, and it will help you to get into the mind of your partner as you can share what they are seeing. If you plan to share your video with other people, this technique will enable the viewers to feel that they are right there in the bedroom with you.

### Creative Techniques

An easy way to add visual interest to your erotic imagery is to shoot footage through a 'mask', such as a window frame. This creates a kind of keyhole effect by masking off areas of the image.

Another way to shoot a scene creatively is to capture part of the action in reflections (such as those found in sunglasses, windows, on the surface of water and so on). You could start with a mysterious close-up of the reflection, and then reveal the bigger picture by either zooming out or physically moving the camera back to reveal what is actually going on.

Shadows are also visually interesting, especially when they become longer and deeper during the afternoon and evening. You could show the shadow of someone dancing and stripping, or of people actually having sex. By showing what is going on without actually showing all the details, you create suspense and anticipation that gets the grey cells going, as well as the libido. For me, this is a very important part of erotica and sex.

### Handheld Camera Moves

Rather than shooting a sequence with lots of static shots from different angles, you can choose to shoot elegant camera moves that I call the 'flying eye'. You need to use a wide-angle lens and move in close physically to get a smooth rather than shaky handheld shot. To allow smooth editing, the best way to do this is to start on a meaningful static shot that you hold for at least three seconds; then you move the camera over your subject, and at the end of the move hold the camera still again for about three seconds. For example, you start showing a foot moving between the sheets, then you reveal more, and then you move the camera over the man's leg and hips, across his chest, and finally on his blissed-out face. The movement has to be very smooth. It helps if you stabilise the camera with both

### Talking Technical: Pulling Focus

*For this technique you have to set the camera to 'manual focus'. You start recording a shot that is out of focus, and then turn the focus ring on the lens until the image is sharp – and all the while keep recording. It is advisable to record the shot for about 15 seconds from beginning until the end: record five seconds out of focus, five seconds going into focus, and five seconds focused. You can also reverse this motion by starting*

*with a focused image and then going slowly out of focus. Going in or out of focus is a good technique to use for introductory or end shots of a sequence. You could go out of focus at the end of a sequence, which provides a very soft transition into the next sequence. It can also suggest a time lapse or introduce a change in location.*

Don't just hang back and watch – hold the camera in your hands and get closer to the action.

hands, hold it at chest level, and keep track of what you are shooting by checking the viewfinder/LCD monitor. Make sure that the take is about 25 seconds long, stays focused and properly lit throughout, and has striking first and last images.

Combining these moves with static shots in the postproduction helps to create a more dynamic and exciting film. By moving physically close to someone with the camera, rather than zooming in from a distance, you make the viewer part of the action. This is particularly true when you film each other during sex.

When you do handheld camerawork, try to walk softly and smoothly, and breath very gently,

as this will affect the steadiness of the camera. If you are walking backwards, check beforehand that there are no obstacles.

Whenever you move the camera – either a 'pan' (horizontal move) or 'tilt' (vertical move) on the tripod or a handheld – always begin and end with a static shot, which should be held for at least two seconds. This will make editing much easier, as it gives you a couple of frames at either end to dissolve in and out from. It is also useful when shooting camera moves to do a couple of takes that vary in direction and speed, so you have a choice when it comes to editing.

 **PRACTICAL TIP**

**Handheld camerawork is a great way to get up close and personal and create the illusion that the viewer is right there in the bedroom, rather than watching from a distance. In the quirky and creative porn film _Slide Bi Me_, handheld camerawork helped to turn a low-budget flick into a bit of a cult hit. The cameraperson really looks like they are part of the action, rather than just observing and directing from a distance. The long handheld takes also reveal just how much all the performers enjoyed themselves.**

## On-set Etiquette

If you shoot in someone else's house or apartment, be aware that it is their home and not just a set for your film. Do not move anything without permission, and before you move something take a Polaroid or digital still of where things used to be, so that you can put everything back in order after the shoot.

Work out how long the shoot will take, then double it and book the location for that period of time. It is better to leave a location early than to run late and be forced to leave without finishing. It is also a good idea to get liability insurance in case you break something during a shoot.

Don't be afraid to stop the shoot if you realise that your tape is coming to an end or the technical quality has deteriorated (overexposed visuals, for instance). Unless something really crucial happens that you could not capture again, it is best to stop filming for a minute and start again when you are happy with the technical quality of what you are shooting.

Before you pack away the camera gear and lighting kit, take a moment to reflect on whether you have got all the images you need to create a sequence that will work when it comes to editing. If you realise that one or two key shots are missing, now is the time to get them.

Push down the 'save' button on any tape you have recorded onto, so that you don't accidentally record over your precious rushes. It's a great help in the edit when you know what's on which tape, so get into the habit of labelling all your tapes immediately after your shoot.

 **PRACTICAL TIP: IN BETWEEN SHOOTS**

**As soon as you can, and definitely before you start your next shoot, review the previous footage on a big screen (such as your TV or a computer monitor) to check the quality and learn from possible mistakes. You will not be able to see a true reflection of the quality (exposure, focus, etc.) of images you have shot on an LCD screen, especially if you are shooting outdoors.**

# BEYOND SHOOTING
## How to Direct

Creating a great sexy movie is not just a case of you and/or your partner learning to be technically proficient with a video camera. If you are the one filming your partner, you also need to be able to direct them – 'stiffness' is an important part of porn, but it shouldn't refer to your performance…

A level of direction is needed even if there is no acting and dialogue involved in your video. Someone needs to be responsible for making decisions on how to shoot things, and they need to be able to get this idea across to whoever is in front of the camera.

Great films often look as if they have been shot unobtrusively, and have a 'fly on the wall' feeling. What you don't see, and often cannot imagine, is that even during the most passionate embrace someone behind the

camera was yelling 'That's great, keep it going!' or 'OK, now kiss and then change positions.' The director needs to know what he or she wants in their movie before the shoot: the must-have shots, how the scenes will be lit, and the way in which the whole thing will be edited together.

**The Bigger Picture**
Somebody has to have the overview, even if it is just the two of you filming each other. You need to have a concept and follow it through. You will have fun doing this, but you have to be aware that having sex on camera is a different experience to just having sex. The excitement will come from the possibility of capturing your chemistry on film and then watching it back later. It can be a very sensual and empowering experience to watch yourselves having sex – it is something that you might have gotten a glimpse of if you ever had sex in front of a mirror.

You might be surprised by how turned on you get by watching yourselves have sex, rather than anonymous porn stars or plastic-looking celebrities, who basically just get paid to do a job. There are many rewards – all you need to do is stay focused during the shoot, and apply your skills as cameraperson and director.

**Interaction and Self-Expression**
No matter whether you are shooting a portrait of your partner or filming them during sex, you need to get a feel for directing your 'model'. Allow your partner to share their many faces with you. Don't force them to smile or laugh all the time (or, in case of glamour photography, to pout or suck on their index finger). This is exactly why some people hate to be photographed or videoed – they feel uncomfortable pretending to be someone that they are not. Let them be playful with their expressions; when you direct them into poses, make sure

these reflect who that person really is. More than anything, if your model is your partner, enjoy discovering and capturing the many faces and facets of their erotic persona, even though you think you have seen them a million times before. If you direct, be specific as to what you need for the picture – for example, tell them to 'arch back and close their eyes' rather than to just 'look sexy!'

## Being Assertive

Directing sometimes means asking whoever you are filming to do things over and over again, so that what they are doing looks just right on camera. If you are patient and supportive, rather than rude and bossy, you tend to get what the film needs.

However, don't make the opposite mistake and not direct because you want to be nice and not make too many requests – you might regret your lack of assertive directing if, for example, you look at your photographs later and discover that there is not a single one that you both just love. You might equally despair if, during postproduction, you realise that you don't have a usable take of a crucial shot. If something is not

quite right, change the camera settings, or the light, or the position of the model to make it better. This way you will increase your options, and ultimately make the effort more worthwhile.

The more you shoot and review your footage with a critical eye, the more you will learn from your mistakes. If you implement what you have learnt, you will become a more confident photographer and director, which will help to bring out the best in whoever you are shooting. If you know what you want, you are more likely to get it – from your camera, your model and yourself.

# VIDEO EQUIPMENT
## The Tools of the Trade

Getting out your 'tackle' for the first time is always a nervous moment – is it too big, too small, do you know how to use it properly, will she laugh at you if you fail to press the right buttons? There's a huge range on the market, and this section gives you the lowdown on what's what.

### Analogue Systems

There are some advantages to using analogue recording devices. It is easy to play the footage back and do some simple assemble editing between the camera and the recorder, for example (although if you do not have an edit control panel, the editing will be very rough).

### ▶▶ VHS:

The fact that you record directly onto VHS tapes (which are the same as those used in a standard VCR), and the fact that the tapes themselves are quite large, means that the cameras tend to be big. As a result, handheld work is difficult, and the tapes also take up a lot of storage space. Another drawback of this format is that the visual quality is very poor compared to digital formats. If you would like to shoot and direct a beautifully lit film, it seems a waste to shoot it on this format – in fact, VHS is pretty much outdated in this digital age.

VHS cameras are very cheap, but it will soon be hard to find spare parts for them, as the technology is becoming obsolete.

### ▶▶ S-VHS:

The S in S-VHS stands for 'super'. S-VHS is superior to standard VHS because it records the sound and images onto different areas of the magnetic tape, and also records the sound in stereo. S-VHS used to be a highly regarded domestic format, and is still widely used. However, the tapes are quite hard to find and can be expensive, and the overall quality does not compare well to digital.

### ▶▶ VHS-C:

VHS-C camcorders and the tapes they use are smaller and more lightweight than VHS and S-VHS. The tapes can be played back and viewed on a VHS recorder when you use an adaptor. The cameras tend to have a helpful number of manual options, but once again this format is inferior to digital.

### ▶▶ Video8:

Video8 is another widely available non-digital video format, and was popularised in the mid-1980s by Sony's Handycam system. It is called 'Video8' because of the width of the cassette itself, which is 8mm. The advantages of this system are that the cameras tend to be lightweight, the whole set-up is very affordable, and the tapes are small and therefore easy to store.

If you go for this option, you should bear in mind that the Video8 camera system is a truly non-professional format intended for simple domestic use alone, and it therefore has a limited number of manual settings. The white balance tends to be a preset feature, which limits your creative options, the picture quality is not great, and you cannot edit the analog footage on your computer without an analog capture card, which digitises the camera's analogue audiovisual (A/V) signal.

**Digital Video (DV) Systems**

Digital is the natural successor to analogue formats. It offers a range of benefits for users: speed, superior quality, ease and flexibility of use and so on. The initial outlay can be more expensive than for an analogue system, but the longer-term benefits make it a worthwhile investment.

▶▶ MiniDV:

MiniDV represents the consumer end of the digital-video camera market. The DV system digitises and compresses the video picture and stores it with digitised audio and time data on a 1/4in tape. As the visuals are digitised there are hardly any of the 'drop-outs' (the loss of visual data on a frame, which creates a nasty white line) that are a problem with analogue systems. The recorded time data is accurate up to a frame and therefore makes logging and editing with a non-linear digital system easy. DV cameras are also a lot more sensitive than analogue cameras, allowing you to shoot usable footage even in poor light conditions. This format has largely replaced S-VHS, Video8 and other analogue systems.

The cost of MiniDV equipment has come down a great deal as the format has become more popular, and most of the cameras offer a good selection of manual features. If you are sure which manual controls are important to you in gaining creative control (white balance, shutter speed and so on), buy a camera with these features in mind, rather than just going for a cheaper 'point-and-shoot' model. MiniDV cameras equipped with 3-CCD technology offer extremely good image quality. 3-CCD records each of the main colours on a separate chip (rather than storing all colours on a single chip), which subsequently improves the picture quality. Two manufacturers are currently developing a tape with an integrated memory chip that will store information on your best takes and help the logging and editing of footage.

▶▶ DV–CAM:

sDV-CAM and DVC-Pro are semi-professional DV systems (from Sony and Panasonic respectively). The technology is very similar to that found in MiniDV, with only slight variations depending on the manufacturer. One of the biggest improvements compared to MiniDV can be found in the time-code recording facility, where it is possible to set a specific time code (i.e. it allows you to number tapes) to make editing easier. These cameras tend to be bigger than MiniDV cams, providing room for more manual controls. They also feature bigger and better lenses, and usually have one or two professional XLR audio sockets that allow the use of professional external microphones.

**Choosing a System**

If you are serious about your ambitions as a filmmaker, a DV-CAM is the system to go for. Even though they cost four to five times as much as a MiniDV camera, this investment should prove worthwhile in the long run; as the saying goes, you get what you pay for. The footage shot on these cameras gets used professionally. Most reality-TV programmes have been shot on one, and a lot of porn gets made with them too.

If you plan to invest in one of these systems and would like to publish your erotic films, I advise that you do at least a couple of short courses in camera, sound and lighting techniques. Only when you know what your equipment can do will you be able to use it to your and your film's full advantage. However, if you are just shooting for your and your partner's pleasure, a basic MiniDV camera should be more than sufficient.

**Sony DCR DVD7 Handycam**

*A stylish camcorder that allows you to capture digital video and stills direct to DVD.*

**Sony Hi8 Handycam**

*An easy-to-use analogue camcorder with video Hi8 recording and a range of manual and automatic facilities.*

**Canon ZR300**

*An affordable 'entry-level' digital camcorder that is ideal for the average home user.*

**Sony HDV 1080i Handycam**

*A small and lightweight digital video camcorder that can also be used to take digital stills.*

**Canon XL2**

*A professional-level digital video camcorder with a wide range of manual features.*

**Sony HVR-A1E**

*Records High Definition picture quality onto MiniDV tapes – the most popular format for broadcasting.*

---

 **PRACTICAL TIP: CELL PHONES AND DISPOSABLE CAMERAS**

If all you want to do is quickly record a bit of bedroom fun, don't worry: it's not essential to use flashy, expensive equipment. One cheap and readily available option is a cell phone with a built-in camera. Many of these can be used to shoot short videos as well as take photos. You're not going to win any awards for your work, but at least they're unobtrusive, easy to use and won't get damaged if you throw them over your shoulder in the heat of the moment. For the ultimate in 'use it and lose it', you can even buy a disposable digital camcorder. But be warned: once your video is 'in the can', you'll have to take the camcorder back to the store to get the data transferred to CD. Could be embarrassing…

# LIGHTING
## Get Yourself Seen

**Light is crucial for filming. Obviously you need sufficient light to see the action, but you can also use it to add colour, contrast and character to whatever you are shooting. If you don't have the flawless physique of the average porn star, careful lighting can also be used to hide a sagging midriff or pimply butt.**

### Colour Temperature

You may well have noticed that during different times of the day the light changes colour. At sunrise or sunset it tends to be warm and golden; at midday, bright sunshine is almost white. The difference in the 'colour temperature' of light is measured in kelvins (K). (William Kelvin was a British physicist who lived in the late 1800s. In one of his experiments he lit a block of carbon, which glowed different colours at different temperatures; from red at low temperatures, through yellow, then blue and finally white.)

There are many different colours and colour temperatures in this spectrum. One of the lowest (warmest) points is a candle flame (1000K), and one of the highest (whitest) is a bright sunny sky (11,000K). Average daylight has a colour temperature of 5500K; indoor 'tungsten' lighting is 3200K. Using this fact creatively can really make a difference to recorded images.

## Setting White Balance

In traditional photography, different films are used for shooting in either daylight or artificial tungsten light to make up for the difference in colour temperature. Digital cameras, however, try to compensate for this difference by using a 'white balance' setting.

Put simply, white balance tells the camera what white should look like in any given light. The standard settings in stills and video cameras are for daylight or tungsten lighting, such as ordinary household light bulbs.

Automatic white balance often produces satisfactory results, but in situations where there are mixed light sources (e.g. daylight and tungsten) or in low-light situations (like sunsets or sunrises), the cameras can get 'confused' and choose a setting that does not look as effective.

The solution here is to use your own judgment and set the white balance manually. If in doubt, take the same shot at two different settings and compare the results – you will be surprised by how much difference a change in the white balance can make. Once you've tried a few different options, you can choose the one that gives the right mood and feeling for the images you want to create.

## Ambient Lighting

Where possible, I advise shooting with available daylight only. Indoors, you can shoot near a window, and can also brighten things up with one or two reflectors. These can be used to bounce the light back onto your subject, and help to avoid the trouble of setting up artificial lighting. Sometimes, when the daylight is not sufficient because it is cloudy or you are shooting at night, you will need to use artificial light sources – otherwise you simply won't be able to shoot usable video footage.

Digital cameras have improved in their sensitivity to light, but when it is too dark, they will fail you in two ways. First, the autofocus will not work because it simply cannot 'see' what to focus on. Second, in low light conditions digital cameras generate 'noise', which appears in an image (particularly in dark, uniformly coloured areas) as specks and unwanted interference.

Think of digital noise as the equivalent of the background hiss of analogue audio equipment. The effects aren't dissimilar to what happens with analogue cameras when a particular type of film is used that can produce very 'grainy' images. However, while the analogue version can look quite interesting and 'arty', especially in images shot in black and white, it is just annoying in digital photographs and videos. Therefore, if your camera menu warns you about 'low light', it means that you should add some illumination of your own.

---

### ▶▶▶ PRACTICAL TIP: POSITIONING LIGHTS

**Be careful where you position your main light, and make sure you create exactly the effect you intend. To get flat, even illumination, place the light at the same level as the camera and point it directly at your subject. If the light comes slightly from the side, you get soft shadows and a more interesting, three-dimensional look. You should not light someone from below unless you want to create a spooky scenario; backlighting will create a silhouette; and lighting someone from above gives them an angelic quality.**

---

### Artificial Lighting

If you are shooting in a dimly lit apartment or hotel room, you can always boost artificial-light levels by changing the light bulbs of any existing lamps and increasing the wattage (as long as this is within safe limits – always check). You can also use coloured bulbs to achieve interesting variations and visual effects.

If these lights are not sufficient, my advice it to get a small halogen photographic light, which is lightweight yet powerful and efficient. I work with one of these and attach a 'soft box' to the front – this diffuses the light so that there are no harsh shadows. I also use a professional dimmer that is powerful enough to deal with my 600W lamp. Rather than just being able to turn the light on or off, this allows me to adjust the light manually to exactly the level I would like on the particular set. Combined with a couple of gels (a blue one will turn the orange-looking tungsten light into daylight for the camera, and a brown one creates nice skin tones and a warm atmosphere), this is an affordable and fully functioning basic lighting kit.

There are also some attachments called gobos. They are mesh-like patterns that create interesting textures of shadow and light. A cheap, effective and creative way to imitate what a gobo does is to move a plant such as a palm leaf in front of your tungsten light and work with the created pattern. The darker it is around you, the more effective the

## PRACTICAL TIP: SAFETY

**To light a set professionally with three-point lighting requires skill and experience. Owning a set of three professional photographic lights is expensive, and if you hire them you need to know how to use them safely. It is easy to overload the circuit you are using – photographic lights are very powerful, and if you plug all three into one socket, it is likely that you will blow some fuses and the bulbs of the lamps you are using. They also get very hot, so make sure you only touch them with heat-proof gloves, and always switch them off and let them cool down before you move or dismantle them.**

light, colours and textures you create will be. To achieve a dramatic impact with your light(s) and gels when shooting in the daytime, you therefore need to darken the room completely.

### Three-Point Lighting

If you feel you have exhausted all possibilities of working with one 'key light', you might like to try a professional lighting set-up known as 'three-point lighting'.

Three-point lighting uses: a key light for the main subject, a fill light to lift the shadows created by the key light, and a back or 'rim' light to illuminate the back and head outline of your model. The idea is to give two-dimensional photography or videography as much depth as possible, so that it almost looks three-dimensional. The three lights are all meant to vary in strength, with the key light being the strongest one – the key-to-fill and key-to-back ratio should be 3:2:2 or 3:2:1. Your exposure is set for the key light.

If you would like to develop your own style of lighting or use three-point lighting and other advanced techniques, it is advisable to do a course on lighting for portraits. However, you can adapt some of the principles of the three-point lighting by using your key light

and integrating a reflector or domestic lighting (with or without gels and different-strength bulbs). Don't get too hung up about light diagrams – open your eyes and work with what you've got.

Start with the key light, and then add a couple of additional light effects so that there is some contrast and depth. When the contrast is there and looks good, you can work on the colour by adding gels or, if you're using digital, by experimenting with the white balance. As long as your images are neither underexposed and grainy nor overexposed and flat, you have lit the scene correctly. To create a mood and work with shadows or colours takes practice and creative vision – be playful and experimental, and don't be afraid to move lights around and vary the concept to suit different settings.

## Natural Lighting

Obviously, three-point lighting does not occur in nature, so you need to learn to use one light source creatively if you want to achieve a natural look. Outdoors there is only one light source: the sun. It might reflect off surfaces, or be broken up into patterns by objects such as trees, fences and so on, but it is still the dominant light source. Even in artificial living spaces, three-point lighting is not common – rooms are generally lit by a single bulb or a strip of fluorescent lighting.

Light should be used to enhance the way things look rather than completely change them (unless you go for something dramatic, like high-impact stage lighting). Set your lights, take a step back, and have a look. If you need to, move a light source or even turn it off – less is often more.

## Creative Lighting

Light sources that you ordinarily wouldn't dream of using in photography can sometimes come in handy and be very effective. Flashlight can work well as a mini spotlight, especially if it is the powerful halogen type. An old slide projector can be used to project slides of textures and patterns onto the model's skin or a backdrop sheet. If you don't have any suitable slides, you can use gels in front of the projector lens to colour the light.

### Talking Technical: Using a Monitor

*It is difficult to tell how the light you are creating for your set will look in a photo print or on a TV screen, and camera LCD screens do not give an accurate reflection of what you are recording. If you have the time, it is worth taking some test stills or video sequences so that you can view them on a TV or computer monitor. For shoots that involve elaborate lighting, it is advisable to use an external monitor.*

*Even a small colour TV that fits into the 'monitor out' socket of your video camera will do – you don't have to invest in an expensive portable monitor that was specifically created for video cameras. Whichever monitor you are using, make sure its brightness and colour are set correctly to give you an accurate reflection of what you are recording.*

# SOUND
## Make Yourself Heard

Sound is the overlooked twin of the moving image; something to which most amateurs and many semi-professional filmmakers pay little attention. There are many beautifully shot and edited erotic films, but the poor quality of the original sound lets them down. Hearing the moans and groans is all part of the fun!

### Built-in Microphones

One of the easiest ways to ensure poor sound quality is to rely on the camera's built-in microphone and leave everything in the 'auto' mode. Built-in microphones only produce satisfying sound quality when the cameraperson is near the subject and there are no distracting background noises like other people talking or traffic. They are not selective, and everything within the same radius will record at the same level. Another problem is that they don't have a buffer to filter out wind noise. Obviously, this is a particular problem for outdoor shoots, where dialogue and other intentional sounds are obscured.

### External Microphones

If dialogue is important in your erotic film, you should invest in some external microphone equipment. Even the type that slides into the accessory shoe on top of your camera will record better sound than the built-in variety – it is bigger, better quality and usually comes equipped with a foam windshield.

▶▶ Directional microphones:
I recommend using a directional microphone that records (even from a distance) whatever you point it at. Sounds produced in the general environment will still be recorded regardless of whether you want them or not, but at a much lower level. This results in increased sound quality, especially when it comes to dialogue.

▶▶ Booms:
Most professional directional microphones come with a large furry cover that acts as a windshield, and they are usually attached to a pole called a 'boom'. The boom allows the sound operator to manoeuvre the microphone as near as possible to the subjects to capture the best possible sound quality. You will need another crew member to do this, as it is virtually impossible to operate the camera and the boom at the same time.

▶▶ Radio microphones:
If you really want to splash out on achieving professional sound quality, you might want to invest in one or two sets of radio microphones. These are compatible with the top-range DV camcorders if they have audio XLR (the standard connection for

---

▶▶| **PRACTICAL TIP: MAKING DO**

**If you decide to stick with your camera's built-in microphone – perhaps because of budget constraints – my advice would be not to record any dialogue unless you shoot indoors, where there is little or no distracting ambient noise, and can get really close to the subject. Where this is not possible, just shoot sexy visuals and edit in music later.**

professional sound). The receiver is attached to the camera; the microphones are 'transmitters' that are worn by your performers, or, if they are nude, attached to something nearby. They send a wireless signal via radio waves to the camera.

## Pros and Cons

One of the downsides of attaching an external microphone to the accessory shoe is that you won't be able to use this slot for a camera-top light. The other problem is that it still cannot record good sound quality if your camera is a fair distance away from your subject. To do this you will need an external microphone plugged into the camera via a cable (most professional ones are plugged into an XLR socket, which is standard in audio equipment and also in most semi-professional DV cams). The advantages of using a radio microphone are that they are lightweight and small, and no one needs to operate the boom. Once you know how to set them up and can monitor the sound levels of your camera manually, the sound and the camera can be operated simultaneously. If you don't want to stretch your budget, you can also hire radio microphones from professional film production firms and media colleges, although I recommend you do a basic course in sound recording before using professional equipment so that you get the most out of these expensive but very useful tools.

## Monitoring Sound

If you are serious about the sound quality, no matter what sound equipment you are using, you need to monitor the sound through headphones to obtain an accurate reflection of what is actually being recorded. Through the headphones you will pick up such things as interference from cell phones (which must be switched off during filming) and the humming noise produced by some types of strip lighting. Headphones are necessary for serious sound recording, so make use of them. I usually wear one headphone over my ear and keep the other one free so that I can communicate easily with my models or crew.

You also have to set the sound to the desired level. This shouldn't be too far into the red zone, otherwise the sound can become distorted. Perform a sound check – you need someone to talk for a minute or so at their normal volume, which gives you enough time to get the sound level right.

Once set, don't make any adjustments between sequences; otherwise you end up with a yo-yo effect that will be either loud and distorted, or low and quiet, but never spot-on.

### Talking Technical: Wild Tracks

*Whatever your location – indoors or out – it is important to record what is called a 'wild track'. This is basically the ambient sound on this particular set, without anyone talking or anybody doing anything that causes a noise. Make sure that there is complete silence and record a minute of this particular sound at the beginning of your first tape (with colour bars if your camera has this facility, or simply a shot of the empty set), and then again whenever you change the location. Even if a room seems to be silent, it never really is; it always has a special sound to it, even if you feel you cannot hear it. The wild track will come in handy when you edit your film, because it can bridge gaps between different sequences and make the edits less obvious.*

# 4 ▶▶ SETTING THE SCENE

# PLANNING AND PREPARATION
## Picturing Perfection

Unless you want to achieve the more-than-real fly-on-the-wall look known as 'gonzo' in the porn industry (a style that is far from pretty, and likes to show 'reality', warts and all), you will have to think about how to transform your home, a hotel room or an outdoor location into a film set.

To 'set the scene', you need to know what the scene will be. Who will be in it? What will you or your partner be doing? Are you just trying to capture your natural, normal lovemaking on film, or are you planning to act out a fantasy scenario that might involve dressing up and possibly even role-play?

**Attention to Detail**

Once you know what scene you are shooting and what you want the mood to be, you can choose your lighting, props and outfits. This is not a waste of time – you will quickly realise the true value of this preparation when you play back the footage in postproduction. In fact, planning what and how you are going to

shoot is, in time and energy terms, just as important as the time spent filming and editing it.

It is the finishing touches that give a film sequence a certain style and help to get the mood across for whoever might be looking at it. To make my first erotic film look special, I spent a lot of time hunting for props that had not been used in any other films. Those sexy and stylish props, in combination with the sensual warm lighting and the chemistry of the real-life couple I was shooting, really made the film.

**A Shared Experience**

This is also a phase of the 'production' where you can work as a team. In some cases it is a

good idea if the person who will be doing less of the actual filming or editing has a bigger say in the planning phase. This way, if you make a film about your passion for each other and you would like it to be a reflection of both of you, it will be a true partnership.

Talking about the location, props and outfits you might use can be very exciting – as you start to share each other's fantasies and create dream scenarios, you might venture into previously unknown territory. So, enjoy the process of getting ready for the shoot; enjoy the magical transformation of an ordinary room in your house or apartment into a film set, and of yourselves into your very own porn stars.

**Get things right off-screen, and what you see on-screen will be all the more successful.**

# THE BEDROOM
## Using Your Love Den

Given that it can be intimidating to strip off for the camera for the first time, the bedroom is an ideal room in which to begin an erotic shoot. Not only is this where you tend to be most comfortable taking your clothes off, it is also likely to be the place where you are most used to being sensual with your partner.

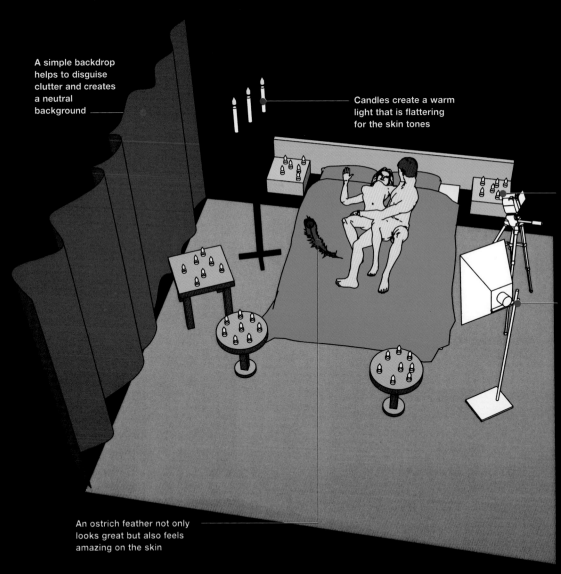

A simple backdrop helps to disguise clutter and creates a neutral background

Candles create a warm light that is flattering for the skin tones

An ostrich feather not only looks great but also feels amazing on the skin

If you would like to turn your bedroom into a film set, you need to de-clutter it. A backdrop can help to cordon off from the rest of the room the area you would like to shoot in. I recommend splashing out on satin or silk sheets that feel and look great.

Candles are a good way to create warm, romantic ambient lighting, but used alone they will not provide sufficient light for filming. To boost general light levels, I recommend using a tungsten light with a brown-coloured gel attached.

Placing the camera on a tripod will ensure that you get steady shots of the action

Attaching a brown-coloured gel to the front of the tungsten light will enhance the candle-lit atmosphere

## TOP TIPS

To give your bedroom that extra boost for a looming video shoot, and to make it look sexy and stylish on film, it is worth splashing out on some extra props. Here are some suggestions:

- Satin sheets feel great on the skin and look good.
- Fresh flowers indulge your sense of smell, look beautiful, and might come in handy as a soft and fragrant tool to stroke your partner with.
- When filming at night, you might like to add some candles (see panel overleaf for more information about using candles).
- If you like to sensually seduce and pleasure each other, keep an ostrich feather, some tropical fruit (or whatever your partner might enjoy tasting), and possibly a blindfold ready. That way one partner could be pampered and surprised while the camera is rolling.

Remember that these are just suggestions. If you do not like any of the above, do not use them. The outfits you might want to wear (whether it's latex, lace or au naturel) are obviously completely up to you; whatever you feel comfortable in will work.

### Candlelight

Candles make an excellent romantic addition to a set for an erotic movie. Rather than just lighting one, why not get a whole bunch of them? Choose fragrant ones based on a smell you both love – if you're into aromatherapy, you might know that ylang-ylang is an aphrodisiac. If you cannot find candles with an appropriate fragrance, just place a few drops of the essential oil into the melting wax (not the flame though).

Place the candles next to the bed – ideally behind you, so that the camera picks up their beautiful warm glow in the background. Candles create a lovely soft light, so don't overpower them with a harsh spotlight; if you use a tungsten light, do so with the diffuser and a brownish gel attached.

### Technical Considerations

When you start shooting your bedroom activities, remember to have fun and not get too hung up about technology and getting that perfect shot. Just relax and enjoy the ride! Your performing, filming and editing will improve the more you do it. Your video will be sexier if you are both enjoying yourselves, even if the technical quality is not perfect.

If the quality of the finished product is important to you, the main thing to think about is what lens(es) you will use. If you are holding the camera by hand, you will need a wide-angle lens, which will enable you to get sexy point-of-view shots that show what you see. For example, if you are lying on your back and your partner is on top of you, you will be able to show their torso and face. If you shot the same image with a standard lens, you would only see a close-up of their face (or maybe even only a part of their face, depending on how close they are). Also, because you are so close to each other and both moving, it is quite likely that the shot would be out of focus. The wide-angle-lens image will not only show more, it will help you to keep the shot in focus because of the greater depth of field (see page 48) that this type of lens permits.

Lastly, for variety, try to get a couple of very high shots of the action by standing on the bed and shooting down. These shots will be an exciting alternative to the side shots you get from bed level.

---

 **PRACTICAL TIP: CANDLE SAFETY**

If you do decide to use candles in your bedroom set, remember to use them safely. Shooting an erotic movie is a demanding process, and with so many potential distractions, it is easy to neglect the basics. Here are some useful safety tips:

- Place them on heat-resistant surfaces – if in doubt, place them in a glass or metal holder.
- Do not position them near drapes or other flammable materials.
- Do not place them on narrow shelving, and ensure that there is a least three feet between the flame and any overhanging surface.
- Don't lean over them while they are burning, as you may set your hair or clothing alight.
- Extinguish all candles before leaving a room, and never leave them burning while you are asleep.
- Candles can go on smoldering, so double-check that they are completely extinguished.

The kitchen is the place where your meals are prepared, cooked and, perhaps, eaten, so what better place to shoot a sexy scene involving food? Think *Nine and a Half Weeks* and you'll get the idea. Why not fill the fridge with your favourite foods, and then feed them to each other or eat them off each other's most sensitive body parts?

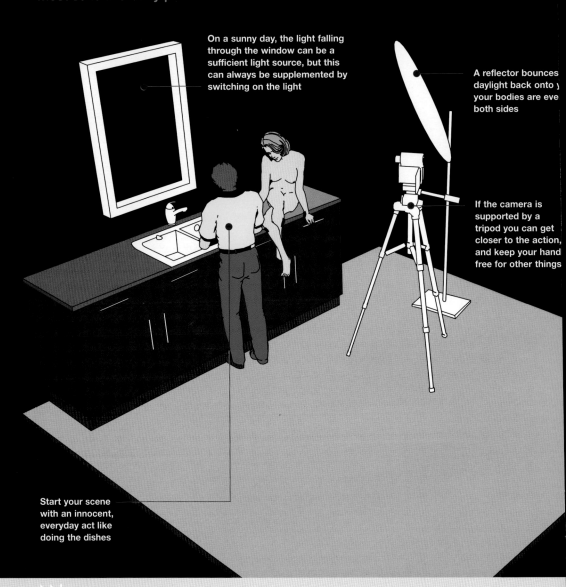

On a sunny day, the light falling through the window can be a sufficient light source, but this can always be supplemented by switching on the light

A reflector bounces daylight back onto y your bodies are eve both sides

If the camera is supported by a tripod you can get closer to the action, and keep your hand free for other things

Start your scene with an innocent, everyday act like doing the dishes

An interesting kitchen-based scenario could be to surprise your partner while they are washing the dirty dishes. Why not try sneaking up on them in your underwear, or even naked, with a video camera in your hand? You could gauge their reaction and, if you get the green light, try to seduce them while filming.

Sometimes it's fun just being spontaneous and going with the flow, rather than shooting a planned and scripted scene. You could swap the camera between the two of you and, if you have a beanbag handy on a nearby work surface, could even put the camera down in order to video both of you together.

## TOP TIPS

- If you decide to use food when filming your video, make sure you've got clean hands. Hygiene issues aside, you don't want to get the camera messy, or so slippery that you might drop it. There are lots of products out there that can be used to wipe your hands on – keep a packet of something suitable nearby throughout the shoot.

- Make sure that all ovens, grills and stoves are turned off – it's all too easy to lose concentration and get burned if your mind is on the action.

- Keep your camera away from liquids, taps and other sources of water – if moisture gets into your camera, it can be damaged beyond repair.

- Work surfaces offer some good options when it comes to lovemaking – their additional height can be particularly useful for certain positions, and for getting a clearer shot of the action. However, it is essential that you test them out first to ensure that they are strong enough to take the weight!

## Technical Considerations

Kitchens are an unusual environment for this kind of work – it's not quite the same as flipping burgers – so there are a few things to bear in mind if you decide to shoot a sex scene in yours:

▶▶ **Lighting:**

If you decide to light this scene artificially, a simple tungsten light with a softbox should suffice. Alternatively, if it's daytime and you have a reasonably large kitchen window, you might be able to catch the ambient light and bounce it back onto your scene using a reflector. Available light is always the most natural-looking option, and in this scenario has the added advantage that you won't have to worry about having an electrical light near a water source. Another plus point of just using available light is that you won't get too hot. You can get sweaty under a bright spotlight, and while that might seem like a sexy idea at first, you will soon start to find yourself gasping for some fresh air.

▶▶ **Camera gear:**

Kitchens tend to be small spaces. If all you've got is a small 'galley' kitchen, rather than a large kitchen/diner, it really pays to use the wide-angle lens. Because it has such a wide field of view, you will fit more into your shots, even though you cannot physically step back. If your kitchen is too small to use a tripod without it getting in the way, this is the time and place for using a beanbag, which stabilises the camera just as well as a tripod, and fits easily into small places.

---

▶▶| **PRACTICAL TIP: PRIVACY**

If your kitchen – or any other room that you use for filming, for that matter – has a window, you might want to give some thought to the issue of privacy. In order to admit as much light as possible into the room, the temptation is to leave the drapes, blinds or whatever open. However, you need to ask yourself if you can be seen from outside. It's best to be cautious – even though you might find the chance of being watched and/or caught in the act an additional turn-on, your neighbours (especially if they have kids) are likely to be less than impressed.

# THE BATHROOM
## Creating a Steamy Scene

Water can really enhance an erotic movie – it feels good on the skin and helps get you relaxed, and it also looks great on film, giving the skin a slippery, shiny appearance. The bathroom is the perfect place to experiment with water, and you can also try out a selection of soaps, oils, creams, foam baths and whatever else turns you on.

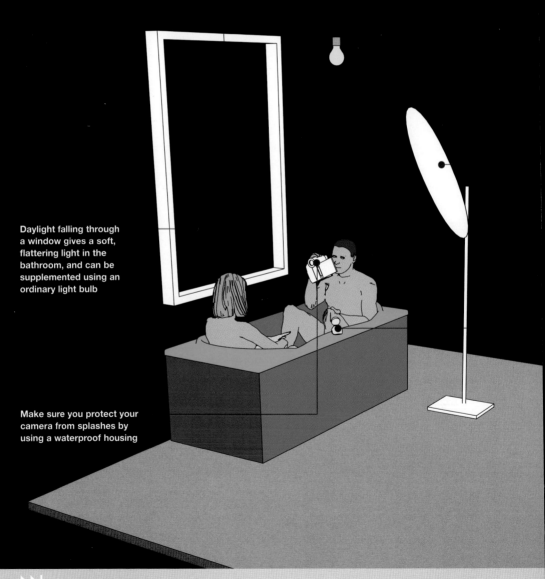

Daylight falling through a window gives a soft, flattering light in the bathroom, and can be supplemented using an ordinary light bulb

Make sure you protect your camera from splashes by using a waterproof housing

The bathroom is a great location for getting intimate with each other. Skin always looks good on screen when it's wet or partly covered by foam bubbles. You could also use scented oils make the experience all the more sensual. If you are feeling adventurous and would like to try something fun and a little bit kinky, try using a selection of waterproof sex toys.

A reflector bounces the light back onto you, so you are evenly lit from both sides

Waterproof sex toys are a key prop for adult fun in the bath

**Essential Safety**

Before you even begin to consider filming each other for a hot shower or bathtub scene, a word of warning. Water is one of the biggest 'enemies' of electronic equipment. Your camera gear will not cope well with condensation, nor will it 'forgive' splashes, which have a tendency to sneak their way into the circuit board and cause irreversible damage. You must also consider your own safety, and avoid anything that could lead to accidents.

## TOP TIPS

Some ideas for getting the best out of your bathroom:

- Flower petals look, smell and feel gorgeous. Rose petals are a good option, and even the petals from wilted roses are perfect. You can scatter them around the room, or fill the bathtub with water and scatter them on the surface.

- One common option if you are shooting a scene that involves taking a bath is to use foam, but for something a bit different try adding food dye. You can use any colour of the rainbow – just be sure to clean the tub immediately after your session, and it would probably be a good idea to take a shower to wash it off.

- If you have a shower with a glass door or a see-through curtain, you can shoot some very exciting video footage or photographs of your partner. This is a particularly good option if you don't have a waterproof camera.

 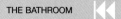

## Protecting Your Gear

Before you shoot in the bathroom, decide how wet you are going to get and how close you would like the camera to be to the action. If you are having a bath or shower together and you want the camera to be right there, you need to protect it. Affordable plastic cases (and I mean proper housings, rather than a plastic bag) are available for both stills and video cameras. Most of the affordable ones are splash-resistant and waterproof up to a depth of 25 feet, which is more than enough. This means your camera can come into the tub with you, and you can also use it to shoot shower scenes.

If you know how to snorkel or skindive, this also gives you the opportunity to get exciting underwater body shots of your partner. If you have sex in the bathtub and dip the well-protected camera under the water, you can get some exciting close-ups.

## Let There Be Light

Once your camera is safe in a splash-resistant or waterproof housing, the next step is to make sure that you use only available light in the bathroom – this means either daylight from a window or artificial light from existing light bulb(s). If you are shooting in the daytime, use a reflector to bounce the light that falls in through the window back into the room. If your bathroom has no daylight, chose the brightest bulb(s) possible for the original light fittings (but never exceed the recommended wattage), and this can be supplemented with a selection of candles.

Remember: you do not want to risk having a big, bright, powerful halogen spotlight near a bathtub that is filled with water when you are in it – it simply isn't safe and shouldn't even be considered.

## Ideas for Bathroom Scenes

With all the technicalities out of the way, you can think about being playful. Here are some ideas that you and your partner could try out for a steamy sex scene:

▶▶ Shower scenes:
Why not film your partner soaping and washing him- or herself down? If you are shooting through a glass door or see-through curtain make sure you set the camera to manual focus so that you focus on the person behind the glass rather than the glass itself. Also remember to get a variety of shots when doing video, such as: their hands washing different body parts, their face in profile covered with running water, and some nice slow sweeps all over your partner's body. This range of shots will allow you to edit the sequence effectively.

▶▶ Filming your partner:
It might be exciting to do a shoot without stepping into the shower with them, and then later look at the footage together. This is a classic example where one of you can become their partner's pin-up. You can shoot images of each other naked, which is the first step to filming each other while making love – it helps both of you to gain confidence in front of and behind the lens (depending which role you choose to take for this particular scenario).

▶▶ Sexy toys:
How about getting some sexy waterproof vibrating toys for each other? Waterproof vibrators come in all shapes and sizes, but I have two favourite toys that double up as props. One is a rubber duck that looks perfectly normal and innocent but has a beak that vibrates; the other is a pair of rubber gloves whose tips vibrate in three different intensities. The gloves are completely waterproof and feel amazing, especially on wet skin. Why not surprise your partner with some good vibrations during a relaxing bath and catch the action on film?

# THE LIVING ROOM
## Love on the Couch

The living room might not seem like the most obvious place to film a scene for an erotic movie, but it does have some advantageous characteristics. Not least, it is likely to be the most spacious room in the house, so it should be easy to light, and you might be able to set up a backdrop. It should also allow greater freedom of movement for yourselves and the camera.

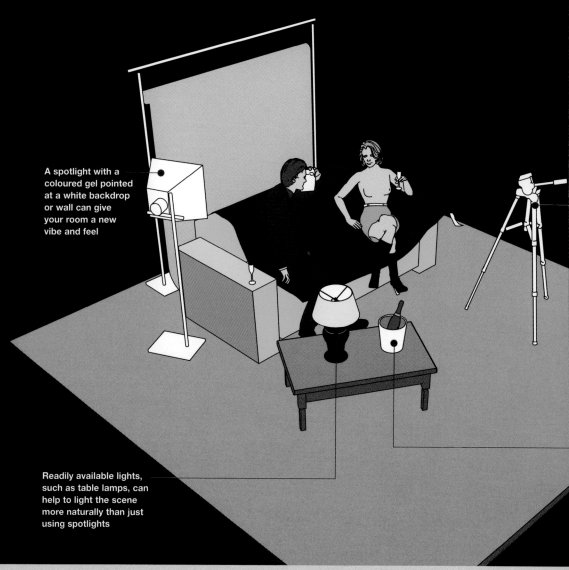

A spotlight with a coloured gel pointed at a white backdrop or wall can give your room a new vibe and feel

Readily available lights, such as table lamps, can help to light the scene more naturally than just using spotlights

Now we come to that all-important question: does size matter? Well, in the case of the living room it certainly does. Because of its generally large size, this room gives you the best chance of creating a movie set. By lighting a plain white wall or photographic backdrop with different colour gels you can completely change the ambience of the room and design a unique and impressive background.

Remember to clear away any clutter – dirty coffee mugs won't look too hot on screen. You could also remove all non-essential items of furniture so you have the space to move around freely, without stubbing your toe on the magazine rack.

Why not splash out on some special outfits and unique props, such as a champagne bucket and glasses, for your big performance? You could also vary your location within the room. Some shots could be taken standing in front of the backdrop, then you could move onto the couch in order to video each other close-up with the handheld camera.

**Keep a tripod handy in case you would like to do some hands-free shots of the both of you together**

**A champagne bucket and some stylish glasses are simple props that look good and feel special to use**

### PRACTICAL TIP: FANTASY OUTFITS

**Dressing up for each other can also be great fun. If you are not sure what to wear, look for inspiration at a local store where you can hire fantasy outfits. Hiring generally makes more sense financially than buying, but if you have a favourite accessory that you feel really suits you and you like using again and again, it makes sense to buy it. I have an extensive dressing-up box, but there are three particular items that I find indispensable: satin gloves, feather boas and a top hat.**

**Ideas for Your Living Room**

This is a sequence where you could produce something really special. There is plenty of space in the average living room, so it's just a case of getting creative and applying skills that you have practiced previously.

▶▶ In da club:
How about giving the set a nightclub feel? If for some reason you can't shoot at night, shut the blinds and use the overhead lights plus a halogen light with a pink gel attached to it. You could also attach a diffuser to the halogen light if you don't want harsh shadows, or leave it off if you would like to work with some shadows for added dramatic impact. A white backdrop would be ideal for either of you to dance or strip for your partner. If you have a couch that looks a bit worn, just use a satin throw to make it look more neutral and classy. If you like champagne, you might want to splash out on getting a proper champagne bucket and stand – it looks great, and drinking champagne from one always feels special.

▶▶ Working a theme:
If you have chosen a theme – say, 'Moulin Rouge' – you can surprise each other in your chosen outfits on the night. Once you are dressed up, the backdrop and light are set up, and the champagne is chilled, go through your list of must-have sequences and have your tripod ready for some shots of both of you together. Then sit back and enjoy your partner stripping for you. Film them with a handheld camera, which you could share with them so they can film you watching (and possibly getting progressively undressed and turned on yourself). When the action heats up, and your hands are full (with each other), place the camera on the tripod.

▶▶ Self-expression:
As always, these ideas are only suggestions. You might like your man to strip for you in a fireman's uniform, or you might prefer not to strip for each other at all. The trick is to enjoy what you do, create a visually exciting set, and then just go with the flow!

**Using Backdrops**

A white backdrop would be ideal if you want to dance, and possibly strip, for your partner. The white area is like a blank canvas you can paint on with light. You can use any colour you like, depending on the type and colour of gel you are using. You could also use a slide projector to project images onto the backdrop and use it like a screen. Slides that show abstract patterns (such as sunlight reflected off water, or clouds in the sky) look great. If someone is near the backdrop, the projections will fall onto their body, and if they are naked this can look amazing. I once did a shoot where I projected images of animal fur onto faces and naked bodies.

As a third option for the white backdrop, you could always light it with a spotlight (with or without coloured gels) from behind. Then you could ask your performer to dance or strip while you film their silhouette from the other side. I have used this technique many times, and the result is amazing – by showing only a silhouette, you create mystery and sexy suspense because the audience fills in the blank spaces with details from their imagination.

A black backdrop is neutral and abstract, but you cannot light it to create a specific mood. If you don't want to use black or white, you can always buy a patterned fabric and drape it artistically over a stand.

 **TOP TIPS**

- Transform your living space into a sexy location by clearing away clutter and carefully placing selected props that all tie in with each other.

- Be experimental with your lighting and try different coloured gels or projections onto a white backdrop (or a wall) to create a unique atmosphere.

- Try lighting and shooting silhouettes for mystery shots.

- Be inventive and shoot from different angles – for example, use a stepladder to get a bird's-eye view of your scene.

# THE OFFICE
## Bringing Your Work Home

Office scenes evoke some familiar associations – a classic office-sex scenario would revolve around the woman in a pencil skirt, rimmed glasses and very high heels, and a guy in a shirt, tie and smart suit. For a twist on this theme, you could make the woman the boss rather than the secretary. You could even have the woman in the suit and the guy in the pencil skirt – it's your choice entirely.

Placing the camera on a beanbag (not tripod) will allow you to get closer to the action and capture some unusual angles

Dressing up can help you to get into character for role-play

The small space provided by a typical home office might not offer a great deal in the way of beds and couches, but it is the perfect location for some sexy role-play. Use your outfits and props creatively. The desk is a perfect item of furniture for bending your partner over in case you would like to do some light spanking or other something similar. The fact that there is no bed or couch in sight might create a bigger turn-on, as it will limit and liberate your sexual activities at the same time.

**Use a reflector positioned to bounce light coming in from the window**

**Props like a desk, computer and eyeglasses will help to create an instantly recognisable office set**

## Location, Location

If you are lucky enough to have a home office, study or library, that's great; if not, and you would like to create a 'sex in suits' scene, you might have to hire one for the occasion. The average home office or study is quite small, so this might be the classic scenario where there isn't enough space to set up a tripod. Should this be the case, it makes sense to use a beanbag to rest the camera on, rather than just shooting everything handheld. By using a wide-angle lens, you will be able to bring the camera in real close. A beanbag will help you to place the camera somewhere suitable – on a desk, for instance – and position it at the angle you need.

### PRACTICAL TIP: PROPS

If you think you might enjoy the office scenario, try to get hold of some authentic props that you could incorporate into the story. They needn't be anything elaborate or expensive – a pencil sharpener, a coffee mug with a cheeky slogan and some stationery would be enough to great an appropriately office-like impression. If you're stuck for inspiration, watch the film *The Secretary* – a very sexy award-winning film that is, as the name suggests, set in an office environment.

## Lighting

As far as lighting is concerned, confined space could make a halogen lamp impractical, in which case use a reflector to bounce some light into the room from a window. This could be combined with available lighting, such as a desk lamp. A blue gel could be handy, because it will keep all the light on this set at one colour temperature – i.e. daylight – rather than mixing daylight, tungsten and other types/temperatures of light.

## Office Scenarios

The office is the perfect location for a boss/secretary theme. You could let one person have all the power and the other one could be the rebel who finally submits to being 'punished' by the stern boss.

▶▶ Domination scenarios:

These scenarios are ideal for a dominant/submissive role-play. You could get dressed up and into a character at first, and then drop the chosen roles and be yourself again when you have sex.

▶▶ Boundaries:

If you engage in this sort of play, make sure you have both agreed what your boundaries are and have also chosen a 'safe word' that means 'game over'. This will come in handy if you truly want to stop and aren't just pretending that you want to be freed even though you actually enjoy being tied up. It is also great fun and very enlightening to 'switch'. Thus, in a different scenario the partner who played submissive is now the dominant one. This way both

partners get to experience each role, and you can imagine what your partner feels.

▶▶ Role-play for beginners:

If you have never dressed up or role-played before, you might want to do it a couple of times before you attempt to film the action. Wait until your roles are more familiar – by then you will be more comfortable in front of the camera and more confident that you can 'act' and shoot at the same time.

---

▶▶| **TOP TIPS**

- **Incorporate suitable outfits and props that might enhance role-play. A tie could become a great blindfold or improvised handcuffs.**
- **If you decide to use some gentle tying up, don't make tight knots that could cut off blood flow, and only use materials that do not cause friction burn.**
- **Establish some boundaries and a 'safe word' if you plan to use domination and submission techniques in your office scenario.**
- **Engaging in role-play requires trust and a good sense of humour. Experiment and enjoy without taking it too seriously. This might be a way to discover and explore your most intimate fantasies.**

# OUT AND ABOUT
## Love in the Great Outdoors

Outdoor sex is great if you like to feel the sun on your skin and wind in your hair when you come. The ideal location is your own garden or back yard – assuming it has a suitably secluded spot where you can indulge in your sensual play without fear of being overlooked.

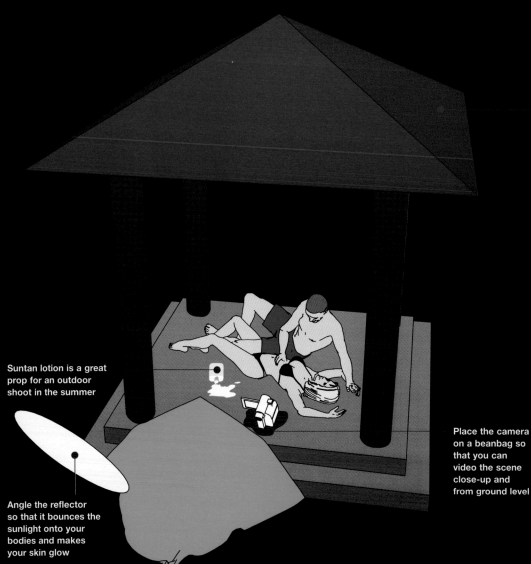

Suntan lotion is a great prop for an outdoor shoot in the summer

Angle the reflector so that it bounces the sunlight onto your bodies and makes your skin glow

Place the camera on a beanbag so that you can video the scene close-up and from ground level

It is a special experience to play sensually in an outside location. The sun on your skin will feel and look great, and you can even work on your tan while you're at it! An outdoor scene is relatively quick and easy to set up. All you need is a reflector to angle sunlight into the shady bits for even exposure, and a couple of sheets to attach to a marquee, tree or outbuilding to guarantee your privacy.

A back yard tends to give you heaps of space and freedom, without the clutter of a furnished room. The cult movie *Slide Bi Me* was filmed almost exclusively outdoors, which made it a very affordable and quick production to shoot (no locations had to be scouted, rented, dressed or lit). A few simple props such as a bottle of suntan or massage lotion should get you going.

**A marquee is an affordable way to create some shade and give you some privacy. Sheets can be attached to the back and sides to block out prying neighbours**

### ▶▶ PRACTICAL TIP: PROPS

As you will be low on the floor on towels or a big sheet, this is another scenario where the beanbag will work really well for getting the camera close to the action – it would certainly be a lot more effective than a tripod. Even on its lowest setting, a tripod would not be low enough; tilting the camera down to compensate potentially creates all sorts of unwanted side effects, such as altering the perspective.

## Staying Within the Law

Many people are nudists – myself included – and view this as a completely valid expression of carefree, natural behaviour. Unfortunately, there are few places in which public nudity is legally acceptable. Outdoor sex is another thing entirely – it won't appeal to everyone, nor is it legal. If you have sex in a public place and someone spots and reports you, you could get into a lot of trouble – even more so if you are videoing what you are doing.

If you have a garden or someone has allowed you to use theirs, make sure that no one from the street or neighbouring houses will be able to peek in. Be creative in making an outdoor set safe and private – you could use an open gazebo, for example, which would give you a roof but still keeps that open-air feel.

## The Light Fantastic

So, given the legal problems and privacy issues, why go to the trouble of shooting nude images or a scene for an erotic movie outdoors? Well, the fact is, done correctly and legally, the results of an outdoor shoot can be worthwhile. Filming outside on a hot and sunny day will not only feel great, it will also look great. There is simply no light quite like sunshine – I call it 'liquid gold', and wish it could be sold in cans because it transforms people with its golden glow.

I'm not talking about the bright, harsh light that you get in the middle of the day. When I talk sun, I mean an early morning or late afternoon glow that flatters the skin and bathes you in gold. After sunrise and before sunset the sun is low, so there are no harsh shadows, and the light also has a 'warmer' quality. It is so powerful that even when you are under a tree or in a gazebo, if you catch the sun and bounce it back onto what you are filming with a reflector, the light won't just be sufficient – it will be perfect.

## Outdoor Scenarios

If you're lacking inspiration, here are some ideas for outdoor lovin' to get you started:

▶▶ The minimalist approach: A perfect outdoor scenario would not need many props: two or more playful people in swimming costumes, a bottle of suntan lotion and a bowl filled with brightly coloured ices chilled in ice cubes. You can rub and massage each other with the suntan lotion – but make sure you wipe your hands before you do any handheld shots.

You can use the ice cubes to get each other's nipples erect, or you could slide them all over your bodies. The contrast of hot and cold will feel amazing on your skin, and ice melting will look great on camera. And the ices... well, you can use your own imagination there!

▶▶ The underwater approach: If you have access to a pool, you can really play. Provided your camera kit is appropriately protected from splashes (see page 90 for more), you can shoot reflections of each other in the water. To do so, set the camera to manual focus, otherwise it will focus on the tiles of the pool. You could also shoot your partner jumping into the water, and then swim around above and below each other to create a full-on aqua-sex sequence.

▶▶ The lifesaver approach: A final classic scenario is the lifeguard. One of you could be a lifeguard who rescues the other with the kiss of life, and things could develop from there. Think *Baywatch* for adults only!

# 5 ▶▶ STILLS PHOTOGRAPHY

# USES OF PHOTOGRAPHY
## Why Shoot Stills?

Given a choice between shooting stills and creating a video, I always choose the photo session first. My advice to couples who want to create sexy visuals of each other is to do the same. The reason is simple: photographs are a lot easier to create for an inexperienced model and/or cameraperson than a video.

**Where to Start**

To create good stills, one ideally has a 'good eye' for composition, framing and the use of light. One should also know basic technical skills, such as the use of wide-angle or telephoto lenses, the difference between using slow or fast shutter speeds, and the effect of different apertures.

Once these skills are learnt, they can easily be transferred to creating videos. The process of weaving a visual tapestry out of moving images that all have to connect in order to 'work' is much less daunting for someone with a trained eye and a mastery of some basic technical skills.

### What Makes Stills Easier

It is a lot less daunting psychologically for the model(s) to be photographed rather than videoed – especially nude. Photos do not record the matching sound with the visuals, and there are many times in between the actual shooting that model and photographer can just relax and chat – all that really counts is what happens in the split second when an image is being shot. Shooting video, on the other hand, means that you are on-camera pretty much non-stop.

Even though you can view the 'rushes' of a video shoot instantly on a digital video camera, they by themselves do not make a film. You might know what I am talking about if you ever shot hours of video footage on a vacation or at a wedding – you quickly get bored watching tape after tape of rushes. A video needs to be edited to work properly, and ideally also have a soundtrack added to it to tie everything together. Taking photographs can therefore be a lot more satisfying than shooting video, as the results are instant. This is especially true when working with a digital camera, when you can have a look at the pictures on the LCD screen of your camera or quickly download them onto you computer.

### Using Your Photographs

There are many uses to which stills of your partner and/or each other can be put; you can choose all your favourite shots and create a special album, for example. Some of my female customers have done this for their partners, who have been blown away by the surprise. It is one of the most creative and intimate gifts you could give to your partner. A more recent trend is to print photos on canvas and have the canvas stretched over a hand-made frame. This gives your intimate portraits another artistic dimension, and can be especially effective if your shot is creatively lit and/or composed.

You can easily email pictures, upload them to a web page or create a digital slide show. The slide show animates single pictures (depending on the software you may be able to zoom in or out, pan across or rotate your images) into a visual presentation; most software allows you to add titles and music to your images as well. You might want to create this slide show for you as a couple to share only, but if you are open to inviting other viewers this might be an original way to introduce yourselves.

### Talking Technical: Enlargements

*One appealing use for your erotic photographs is to choose your favourite shot and have it blown up as an enlargement, perhaps with a view to framing it. However, there are some limitations here, depending on the equipment you are using. If you use a digital camera, you will need a good-sized sensor (something in the region of four megapixels), and you should shoot at the highest possible resolution setting. If you work with traditional 35mm film, you shouldn't have too many problems achieving a good-quality enlargement, as long as your camera and lens are of a reasonable standard.*

**If an image is this small on your monitor, it isn't large enough to make a decent-sized print.**

# WHAT YOU NEED
## Choosing a Camera

**There are thousands of cameras to choose from. What you get depends on your personal preferences, but there are some questions you need to ask yourself first, such as: what you would like to shoot, how creative you would like to be with manual controls, and how 'instant' you would like the results to be.**

### Film vs. Digital

When you shoot digitally, you have an instant result that you can play back on the LCD screen of your camera or even view on your TV or computer screen. You can see instantly what works and what doesn't, rather than having to wait for the film and prints to come back to spot a huge mistake in lighting or composition you might have made.

It makes sense to own at the very least a basic PC and printer if you use a digital camera. This way you can download the images and work on them using image-editing software, many types of which are currently available. You can crop the images, make them lighter or darker, or even have a play with various creative effects. Try not to rely on image editing too heavily, however. If the composition and lighting are right and it looks great, you can make it look even better in postproduction, but there is little that you can do to save a badly composed or ill-lit shot. If you want to become a good photographer, train yourself to get things right during the shoot, rather than becoming lazy and saying 'I can do it later in PhotoShop'. Staying switched on during the shoot can also save you time in the long run – it's a lot quicker to use concealer on somebody's pimply butt than it is to airbrush it later digitally.

The old school of photography still defends the use of film. The reason is simple: the image resolution provided by even a cheap camera is much better than that of a basic digital camera. This doesn't matter so much if you only want to run off small prints, but it does matter when you enlarge your favourite images. If you blow up a shot that was taken on, for example, a two-megapixel camera, you will see a dramatic decrease in image quality. Do the same with a 35mm negative, and the quality will be fine. The upshot is, if you choose digital and want to 'go big' with your artwork, invest in a camera with a high-megapixel sensor.

### Talking Technical: Back-ups

*As all digital images are stored on a memory card and there are no hardcopy 'negatives' as such, be careful what you select when you view images back. You may want to delete a few images, perhaps to make room on your memory card, but it is possible accidentally to 'select all' and lose a long day or night's work. My advice is to download images onto your computer immediately and then burn a back-up copy on a CD or DVD as soon as possible. This way you are safe, even if your hard drive gets damaged.*

### Nikon CoolPix 5200

*This is a good example of the type of digital compact camera that many people buy for general use. Despite its small size, this camera has a 5.1-megapixel image sensor, which is large enough to obtain good-quality prints up to 20 x 16 in.*

### Canon EOS Digital Rebel

*This is an affordable 'entry-level' digital SLR camera. It offers more features than the average compact camera, including interchangeable lenses, and manual focus and exposure settings. The result is much greater flexibility of use.*

### Canon EOS 1DS Mark II

*At a cost of several thousand dollars, professional-standard digital cameras such as this are beyond to means of the average amateur photographer. If, however, you want to capture images of the highest possible quality, they are worth every cent.*

## Compact vs. SLR

The other debate common in photography circles is whether to get a compact (or 'point-and-shoot') camera or a sophisticated single-lens reflex (SLR) camera. Both cameras exist in both film and digital formats.

▶▶ Compact cameras:
The advantages of a point-and-shoot camera are that they are easy to use, lightweight, affordable and won't intimidate your model(s). The huge disadvantage is that most of these cameras run on autopilot – i.e. they give you few, if any, manual options – and so can greatly inhibit your creative freedom. This gets very frustrating after a while. You might wanted to shoot your partner at night in a romantic, candle-lit setting, but because your camera's flash automatically pops up in low light conditions, you'll end up with a brightly lit image that looks flat and fails to convey the mood of the moment.

If you buy a compact and want some creative control, get one that allows you to choose a manual setting for at least one of these factors: flash, focus and shutter speed. These functions give you a lot of creative control. For example, you will be able to shoot silhouettes at sunset by turning the flash off.

▶▶ SLR cameras:
SLRs are what most professional photographers choose to work with. This kind of camera uses the same lens to view the subject as it does to take the pictures (unlike compact cameras, where the subject is viewed, and the image shot, through separate optical systems). The upshot of this is that SLRs provide a more accurate idea of how your finished picture will be framed. SLR cameras also give you the option to work with separate, interchangeable lenses, allowing you to select a wide-angle, telephoto or zoom lens as appropriate.

Film SLRs have come down a lot in price, and even digital SLRs are becoming affordable for the consumer market. Don't let the size and complexity of an SLR camera intimidate you. They have a huge variety of manual settings that will allow you to choose and handle one manual control at a time and become more creative, but they also have a range of automatic settings that you can use to get yourself familiarised with things.

## Flash

SLRs generally have an accessory shoe (or 'hot shoe') on top of the camera, which allows you to use an external flash As explained earlier (see page 70), external flashes are superior to built-in ones, and are less likely to produce harsh, unpleasant shadows. Modern flashes are very sophisticated – with one button you can change their strength depending on the situation you are shooting in. You can also fully angle and rotate the flash head so that you can shoot the light from various directions.

## Accessories

Whether you go for film or digital, compact or SLR, you will also need to equip yourself with a small kit bag. Here is a run-down of some useful accessories to consider:

(see page 70)

▶▶ **PRACTICAL TIP: PRIVACY**

**If you would like to shoot erotic images, one huge advantage digital has over analogue (film) is that nothing has to be sent to a lab to be developed and printed. Unless you have your own processing facilities, and a darkroom to create enlargements, you will have to hand in your 35mm film to a lab. Depending on the content of the images, this might be a daunting thing for you to do, especially if you don't live in a big city, where it's easier to retain some anonymity. Even though no employee in a lab is legally entitled to distribute the images you shot, you can only trust that they don't run off prints for themselves, or copy your negatives and then later distribute them over the Internet – as has happened to some celebrities that we've all heard about.**

▶▶ Camera bags:

A camera bag will protect your camera from any impact during transport and from the elements while shooting outdoors. Cameras are very sensitive and can easily get damaged by water, grains of sand, too much heat or being shaken about, so do protect them.

▶▶ Tripods:

A tripod is useful for those self-timer shots of you and your partner, and is indispensable for close-up shots (where the depth of field can be so small that it matters if you move even a fraction of an inch) and slow shutter speeds. If you have the

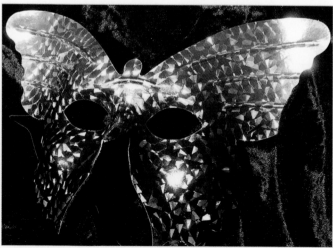

money, it pays to buy a sturdy tripod rather than a lightweight one, because it will remain stable even if you shoot in challenging conditions. If you are planning to shoot video as well as stills you could use a proper video tripod that has a 'fluid head'. This will work for video-camera moves like pans, but is also rock-solid when 'locked off'.

Another cheap but useful item is a small beanbag, which can be used to support the camera in a similar way to a tripod – the advantage being that is easier to transport and can be used to get a lot closer to the action, especially at low angles. You can even make your own – all you need is a zip-lock bag filled with a pound or so of rice or lentils. Be aware of the limitations of this makeshift form of tripod, though: as the camera is not actually screwed on, it could fall off if you are not careful.

▶▶ Reflectors:
A reflector is an affordable 'must-have' prop for photography and videography alike. It is basically a sheet of reflective material, and can come in a variety of shapes, sizes and colours. You use it to catch light and bounce it onto your subject. My favourite reflector is gold on one side and silver on the other – the former creates a warm, flattering glow on someone's skin, the latter a cooler, sophisticated tone. A reflector cannot bounce light over a great distance, but is effective when held near to the subject. If you cannot hold the reflector because you are busy shooting and/or posing, just prop it at an angle against a support.

## Talking Technical: Filters

*An ultraviolet (UV) filter is a must when shooting outdoors. Not only does it protect the lens from scratches, it also makes the sky look a nice deep blue. If you are shooting in really bright outdoor locations you might need a neutral-density (ND) filter that reduces the amount of light entering the lens and will allow you to set a slower shutter speed if you want to.*

*A 'graduated' version of this filter (ND grad) is available, and allows you to balance a scene in which there is one area that is much brighter than another. The classic example for using an ND grad is a scene in which the top portion of the frame is dominated by a bright sky, which you would like to darken to match a less bright foreground. Coloured graduated filters are also available, and come in all the colours imaginable. They are useful if you want to create a dramatic sky from one that looks, in reality, rather dull and grey.*

*If you are planning to shoot around water, or by windows or mirrors, a polarising filter can be handy. With it, you can choose whether you would like to show reflections (in a window or on the water surface, for example) or whether you would prefer to cut out the reflections in order to show what's behind/underneath. By twisting the polariser while looking through the viewfinder, you will be able to see which reflections you could use or lose.*

# CREATIVE TECHNIQUES
## How to Achieve Something Different

The best advice I can give anyone when it comes to creating erotic images of each other is: forget everything you know about glamour photography and pornography. While any couple will discover their own preferences and way of doing things, here are five ideas that can act as jumping-off points.

### ❶ Open Your Eyes

Many of my female customers come to have sensual portraits taken by me because they feel uncomfortable with their partner's attempts to do so. The reason for this is that many men have been brainwashed into a 'glamour' or porn iconography from an early age and have certain images stored in their mind. Everybody is an individual and wants to be treated as one; everybody is sexy in his or her own unique way. Trying to turn your partner into a glamour 'clone' will probably make them feel uncomfortable and tense, and this will show in the pictures.

A person does not have to be naked to be sexy. It's all in the eyes – if the eyes say, 'I am happy with who I am, where I am and what I am doing', they exude confidence, which is usually very sexy. Look at your partner with fresh eyes, give her/him a chance to be themselves, and then try to create images that have never been done before rather than copying what has been done a million times.

A woman photographing a male partner faces a different challenge. While female pin-ups are everywhere, there is no real pin-up culture for women who fancy men. Most male nudity or sexiness is hidden, and sexy photos of men tend to be for other men. This is why men are often paranoid about 'looking gay' when being photographed in sexy poses (not realising that many women actually find gay or bisexual men attractive). Just as much as women do not want to be compared with pin-up clichés, neither do men. As a woman photographing a man, therefore, you have a disadvantage that could in fact turn out to be an advantage: there is so little that you can draw inspiration from, you can start afresh and photograph your man in the way you feel he looks sexiest (as long as he is comfortable doing it).

If you use a self-timer to photograph yourselves while having sex, forget everything you know about porn. Don't get too hung up on certain positions or the 'money shot'; aim instead to take unique images that capture your chemistry and essence as a couple.

### ❷ Use Light and Dark

Traditional glamour photography and pornography tends to be so brightly lit that there often aren't any shadows at all. To me, this is exactly the reason why so many people tend not to find porn sexy: everything is on show; there are no shadows, and therefore no sense of mystery.

I love using the available light alone, rather than a flash or big, bright spotlights; both are too harsh for my taste. If I need a light or two, I deliberately use them so that they create a shadow (maybe on the backdrop behind the model or on certain body parts). To me this is very sexy, as it leaves things to the imagination instead of

giving everything away, and I would like people who look at my pictures to think, 'I wonder what's going to happen next', rather than knowing it all already.

I also like shooting silhouettes – their abstract nature means that you can really focus on someone's profile or body outline, and it is also a great way to shoot a person anonymously. All you need is a bright light source (such as the sun or a spotlight), which should be positioned behind your model. You must also switch off the flash on your camera – if you don't, it will fire automatically and will light up your subject instead of leaving them dark. Lastly, if you are using a slow shutter speed, you will also need to stabilise the camera using a tripod or beanbag.

### ❸ Play with Colour

Another useful creative technique is to use coloured gels when working with spotlights. Gels are translucent, thin sheets of plastic. As well as different thicknesses, they come in all the colours of the rainbow, and are not very expensive. You can also use the gels wrapped around a domestic light – just be careful that the gel never comes too close to whatever bulb you might be using, as the heat of the bulb could melt it. Different colours create different moods: brown gels give a nice, warm skin tone and work well with candlelight; blue is a cold but dramatic colour and can be used at night to create a mysterious feeling; red and pink are extreme colours, but can give great results depending what feel you are after. Experiment with gels – get at least four colours, and each of them in a thick and a thin density.

### ❹ Add Another Layer

Shadows and colours add 'layers' to an image. Rather than looking at a brightly lit image of a nude person, you might try having your partner or yourself semi-naked, lit with a blue gel, with a big shadow behind you – simple techniques that allow you to create a mood and tell a story. Another way to create new layers is to add textures. I am a big fan of shooting through material, and have a wide range that I use stretched over the lens to create a 'keyhole' effect.

I find these 'organic filters' less clinical than using a professional filter, as it is a lot harder for the viewer to tell what is actually going on. Another plus point is that it is easy to change the way you use them – you can hold the material closer to the lens or further away from it, and you can let the material flow loosely or stretch it tightly over the lens. You also have the option of covering all or just part of the frame.

This technique might not work so well if you shoot with a compact camera, as you need to tell the camera what to focus on – i.e. the model in the background rather than the material in the foreground. If you cannot focus manually, the camera's auto setting might ruin the effect.

### ❺ Let it Flow

If you have manual options on your stills camera, you might be able to adjust the shutter speed manually. As we have seen (see page 49), the shutter speed determines how long an exposure is and how much of the action is being recorded. If you shoot at one-thousandth of a second (1/1000sec), the shutter opens for such a short time that the image looks like it is frozen in time. Fast shutter speeds like this (and faster) are used in sports photography – say, for example, that you wanted to photograph a swimmer and capture the detail of individual droplets of water around him or her.

I'm a big fan of using slow shutter speed.s This means that the shutter remains open for longer, and you record more of the action as a consequence.

### Mask Shot 1

This image has been shot through some flexible mesh material in order to give it texture and a sense of mystery.

### Mask Shot 2

A similar technique, but this time the mesh material has been stretched tightly over the lens to create a diagonal pattern.

### Fire Shot

This image was shot with a slow shutter speed of half a second and slow-sync flash, allowing the motion of the flame to show, rather than freezing the action.

### Backdrop Shot

The red velvet backdrop corresponds well with the colour of the flower, and creates an uncluttered, calm, warm background.

### Shadow Shot

This image was lit using one powerful spotlight with a very dark blue gel against a white wall at night. The resulting large shadows and unusual light create an aura of mystery.

### Wall-of-Fire Shot

This was shot against a giant light object creating the illusion of flames. No flash was used in order to preserve the warm skin tones, shadows and startling silhouette.

Slow shutter speeds start from about a one-thirtieth of a second (1/30sec), and can go up to 30 seconds or longer, depending on your camera model.

When you use a slow shutter speed, any movement that occurs while the exposure is being made will be recorded as a image blur. Depending on how fast and in what direction (relative to the camera) your object is moving – for example, during dancing, showering or sex – some part of the person or maybe even all of them will be blurred to a lesser or greater extent.

By leaving the camera on a self-timer, you can experiment with different shutter speeds while making love – you will be amazed at the results you might get. There are no hard-and-fast rules, although it is best to shoot in low light conditions – bright lights will quickly become overexposed during long exposures. You can compensate for this to an extent by using a small aperture, which will let less light into the camera.

One of my favourite techniques is to shoot long exposures at night, using some strip lighting or candlelight combined with a short burst of flash. This creates a unique look – the slow shutter speed will ensure that the dimmer ambient light is recorded, and the flash will 'freeze' part of the action, so that the entire image isn't blurred. If you used the flash without the slow shutter speed you would completely loose the warm glow of candlelight or the candy-colour glow of the strip lighting, so this is a great creative technique to play with if you like to enhance rather than kill the mood in your images.

# 6 ▶▶ POSTPRODUCTION

# EDITING
## The Director's Cut

To me, this is the most exciting part of a film production. You have your unedited tapes – the 'rushes' – which are like pieces of a jigsaw puzzle. Only through the editing process and by giving individual images their place does the whole picture fall into place.

### Editing Systems

There are two main styles of editing: linear and non-linear. The difference between these systems is similar to that between a typewriter and a computer. When using a typewriter, one error could ruin a whole page, but using a word-processing program on a computer you are able to correct mistakes constantly, as well as change the order of paragraphs, and so on.

▸▸ Linear editing:

Linear editing is analog editing: a copying process from one tape to another, very similar to copying a favourite audiotape on your home stereo for a friend. You could edit in this way using a very basic set-up – simply connect your camera to your VCR and press play and record. However, unless you have an 'edit control panel' this is an awkward and fiddly process. Your editing will never be precise to an individual frame, and you will battle with the time delay that both machines have between pressing a button and them actually acting on the command. This is OK for a 'rough cut', but will never be an accurate or smooth way of editing.

This biggest disadvantage of this system is that you can only do one edit at a time, one after another. If you decide five minutes into the movie that you want to take out a shot that appears three minutes into your film, you have to go back and recreate the whole sequence, one shot at a time. Another big problem associated with linear editing is that once you copy the footage (which you have to do in order to edit), you actually lose quality. The degeneration of the footage from one generation to the next is quite significant and the rate of drop-outs will increase.

A good-quality monitor will help when it comes to non-linear editing.

**Talking Technical: Time Codes**

*When you view your footage you need to make a 'time code' list that includes: the tape name and number, the time code in and out (this is to mark the beginning and end of a good scene), a scene description and comments on the scene. Below is an example.*

*Editing programs are available that include logging software, so that you type in the information, rather than writing it down on paper. The advantage is that the computer will be able to grab any selected scenes from the digital tape and transfer them onto the computer automatically based on your log sheet.*

*All you need to do is to connect the DV camera to the computer and use the software to select what you would like to download.*

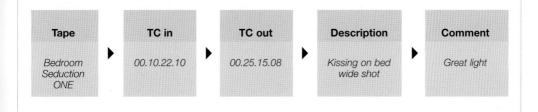

| Tape | | TC in | | TC out | | Description | | Comment |
|------|--|-------|--|--------|--|-------------|--|---------|
| *Bedroom Seduction ONE* | ▶ | *00.10.22.10* | ▶ | *00.25.15.08* | ▶ | *Kissing on bed wide shot* | ▶ | *Great light* |

▶▶ Non-linear editing:
If you have a computer, I advise teaching yourself how to use non-linear editing software. There is a huge range of programs to chose from, and many computers come with user-friendly editing software. Most computers also come with a built-in 'capture card' that allows you to copy digital video onto your hard drive; even if your computer does not have one, affordable versions are readily available.

Non-linear editing means that at any time during the edit you can move shots about, trim their duration or add visual effects. You are truly free to weave a beautiful visual web rather than crawling along snail-like in one straight line. A great advantage of these non-linear editing systems is that they are visual. Rather than just editing 'blind' by time codes that you read from a list and have to wait for the tape recorder to find, you will actually see many small images ('thumbnails') of every sequence. All you do is click on one, and drag it into your timeline. If it doesn't fit where you dragged it, you can move it easily with just one mouse click. You can also do a 'rough edit' to begin with, and then fine-tune things by shortening certain sequences and adding interesting effects like slow-motion shots.

**Edit Preparation**
Just as when shooting your footage, to edit successfully you need to have a purpose and know what you would like to achieve. The most important preparation for the edit suite is to view all your rushes and log them, so that you know what sequence is where on each tape or disk. This is a lot easier if you shoot digitally, as an accurate time code is recorded during shooting, which you can display during playback. Just choose the display option TC in the menu when you transfer your digital tapes onto VHS tapes.

After you have chosen all the best shots and sequences, and have transferred them to your computer, you need to have a concept before you actually start editing. I find that it helps to create this concept on paper. I use note cards of different colours if my film has various chapters –

each colour signifies another chapter in your movie. If you would like to edit just one sequence of yourself making love, rather than creating a film with many chapters, then one set of note cards will be enough. You write the time code and a few key words of each usable sequence on one of the cards. Sit at a big table or on the floor and spread all the cards around you. You are now free to shift the cards around into different orders. This way you can actually do various 'paper edits' that might inspire you to do a real edit later on that you could not have imagined if you had started editing straight away.

It is important not just to think about a visual concept beforehand, but also to choose your music tracks and make sure the issue of copyright is sorted if you plan to publish your film. Do not underestimate the impact of the soundtrack on the film. A lot of well-shot erotic films don't work because of the bad music that has

been pasted over them. Try to choose music with a 'meaning' that ties in with the overall theme of the sequence, rather than 'wallpaper' music. Sometimes it can be quite powerful to use just the original sound. This only works, however, when you have excellent sound quality.

**Editing Styles**

When editing, it is important to bear in mind the general style that you want to use in your movie. There are two main techniques:

▶▶ Chronological editing:
One way to edit is chronologically – that is, to show things in the order in which they happened. Continuity of aspects such as lighting is very important with this technique. If you are shooting your partner stripping, you should show one thing at a time, without leaving anything out. A 40-second sequence would show an establishing shot of him/her walking onto the set, then a

close-up of a glove being pulled off, then a wide shot of the top coming off, then a camera move up him/her that starts on their shoes and ends on their front with the pants coming off. Then you would show the other glove coming off in a wide shot, and so on until they are fully naked.

▶▶ Discontinuous editing:
A second editing technique allows for a lapse of time, and looks more like a series of short clips. You could be adding various different activities/locations in one sequence without being tied down by rules such as continuity and 'crossing the line'. You could show the glove coming off in close-up, then fast-forward in time and cut to the top coming off, then show them naked. This works, providing the shots are all filmed from different angles and framed differently. If they were all framed and shot in the same way, the clip-like edit would just look comical.

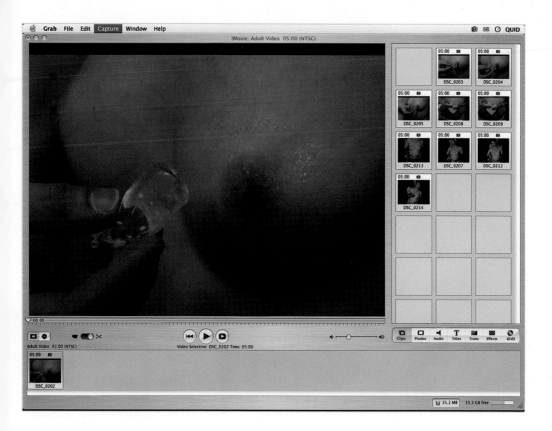

## Shooting for the Edit Suite

When you start to edit you will quickly learn what works and what doesn't, and you will realise that successful editing starts during the shoot. The following tips will help you to shoot for a smooth editing process. You will learn to implement them because there is nothing more frustrating than having great footage that cannot be edited and just sits in your archive gathering dust. Overleaf are my top-ten tips for shooting with editing in mind.

---

### ▶▶| PRACTICAL TIP: RULES OF EDITING

No matter which editing style you choose, always sacrifice everything else for clarity during postproduction. Sometimes there is an amazing shot, but if it does not help to 'tell your story' it is best not to use it. Editing is like building a house (the finished film) out of bricks (the rushes). Some segments fit better than others, and some will always be left over in the end because even though they are solid and colourful building blocks they did not fit into the house you were making.

Expect to edit on average three minutes of film per day if you do relatively fast edits and edit to music. If you use long, slow takes (such as a slow pan that can last up to 20 seconds) and do not edit to music, you can expect to edit about five to six minutes.

❶ Remember to grab an 'establishing shot' – a wide shot that can be used to introduce a sequence or as a neutral in-between shot.

❷ Make sure your shots last long enough. Remember you are not shooting stills but video, so make sure your sequences last at least 10 seconds for static shots and around 20 seconds for moves such as pans or walks.

❸ You need to vary the size of your shots within the same sequence. Get at least three different shots of the same thing – wide, close-up and moving. If everything is framed the same, your edits will 'jump' and look really unprofessional. It looks best when you alternate wide shots with close-ups and statics with moves.

❹ Remember to start and finish camera moves (pans, tilts and walks) with static shots that you hold for at least three seconds. This allows you to edit with slow transitions ('dissolves') if required.

❺ It is important to let people 'leave the frame' when they move past the camera, rather than always following them. The 'empty frame' allows you to edit to whatever you want next and move on with your action.

This way, in the first shot a person may walk out of the house and in the next shot you can get away with showing them in the swimming pool.

❻ When moving the camera, reverse the direction and speed of moves so you have various options that you can use in your final film.

❼ It is vital to get reaction shots. Shoot what somebody does and also the reaction of the other person; even if they just watch and don't do much, this is important to show the interaction between two people. If you film yourself in bed with your partner, you need an establishing shot from the tripod. Then each of you has to film the other person while doing the same thing. Only this way you can fuse the action together later in postproduction.

❽ Shoot as many 'cutaways' as you can. After covering the wide shot, get two or three close-ups of the same action that you could 'cut away' to.

❾ If people are facing each other in a wide shot and you want to show them each separately after your establishing shot, make sure you get an 'eye-line match'. What this means is that if one person looks to the left of the frame, the other needs to look to the right. This way the idea gets across that they are looking at each other, rather than away from each other. The close-ups have to match the wide shot, so make sure you do not reverse the direction in which each individual is looking.

❿ Make sure you do not 'cross the line'. This refers to an imaginary 180-degree line, also called the 'axis of action'. Stay on one side when shooting any shots or cutaways. If you cross the line, those shots will not work in the edit because the viewer intuitively wants to stay on the side where the camera originally was.

 **PRACTICAL TIP: CHOOSING A STYLE**

Knowing how you intend to edit a sequence before you actually shoot it will save you time. If you are planning to edit in a non-chronological clip-like style, just getting some key shots of one of the activities is sufficient. Extra shots are required to create a whole chronological sequence. It helps to know before the shoot how you will edit the sequence so you do not under- or overshoot.

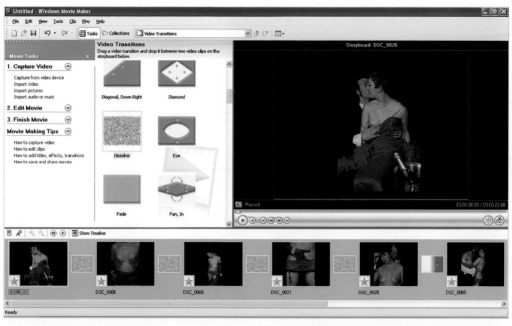

# STORAGE AND ARCHIVING
## The Joy of Backing Up

**Archiving completed work is not top of everyone's agenda, and can seem like a bit of a chore. However, if you've put in the effort and are pleased with the results, you need to make sure that everything is carefully stored – losing original, irreplaceable work is a major let-down.**

### Video

Always label all your tapes during a shoot, immediately after you have used them. If you are using analog, remember to push in the tape's 'save button' so that you will not accidentally record over precious footage. If you have decided to play back footage during a shoot, make sure the end of the last shot on the tape is lined up correctly so that you don't record over footage or create 'holes' in the tape. The latter could lead to a time-code break, which will make viewing and editing a nightmare. Most digital cameras have an 'end search' button that can be used to line up the end of the shot footage to an exact frame.

▶▶ Rushes:
Your rushes are very important. Make sure you handle them carefully, and do not use the originals for viewing – fast-forwarding and especially pausing can crease and damage the tape. Ideally, you only let the original tapes play when you do a transfer onto VHS for logging or onto your computer for transferring the data. It is a luxury (but it might be well worth it if you intend to do a lot of filming and editing) to get either a DV deck or a second DV camera, so that you can copy your rushes. If you copy from DV to DV via a FireWire connection there is no loss of quality and you will get an identical duplicate of your original rushes. You could also do limited edits between the two cameras, and of course use the second camera during a shoot – one camera could be on a wide setting, the other one recording the close-ups, for example.

### Stills

If you shoot onto a memory card, download the pictures from your camera to your computer as soon as possible. As pictures shot in high resolution create large files, you might want to invest in an external hard drive that you use exclusively to store visual data. External hard drives are very affordable, and using one means that your main hard drive will not be slowed down when doing day-to-day applications.

---

 **PRACTICAL TIP: SAVING YOUR WORK**

**If you edit on a computer, remember to save your work as often as you can, so that if the computer crashes you will not lose a lot of valuable work. Many programs have an 'auto save' setting, which is generally set to save at ten-minute intervals. Even so, losing ten minutes of work can be a serious drag, especially if you had been working on fiddly edits and effects. It's best to get into the habit of saving your work more frequently, and it's easy to do if you learn the shortcut code on your keyboard (e.g. Command + S).**

---

## ▶▶ PRACTICAL TIP: FILE NAMES

**Digital cameras automatically give images a file name (usually in the form of a number). It is a good idea to turn off the 'reset file numbering' option, so that each time you shoot new images they will receive completely new file names that are not identical with any of those you have already downloaded. It is easy to get confused if you have two or more images with the same number/name – you might accidentally delete the wrong picture, for example.**

**Make sure you label your storage disks clearly so that you know what's on each one. Try to use a consistent naming system, such as the date in combination with a serial number or letter. This could save you hours of searching time. It is useful to print out thumbnails of all of the images in each folder, including the file names (most image-editing software can automate this process for you). This gives you an immediate overview of what is on each disk, without even having to open it.**

images or video clips. The only drawback here is that you will lose more work if the DVD gets scratched or damaged, so you might want to make two copies and store them in separate places in order to spread the risk.

▶▶ Scanning:

If you shoot on film, you can scan your images to create a digital back-up. Even if you don't have a computer, most photo labs offer this service – as long as you are happy for them to see your images.

▶▶ Cataloguing:

Cataloguing takes place after you download your work. First, make sure you create clearly named folders for each shoot, rather than storing hundreds of images in one folder. If you shoot a lot of images, it makes sense to get a browser program. A range of products is available, including a number of free 'shareware' programs. If you decide to invest in a commercial image database, you will be able to create a professional catalogue and locate your images by search terms. Remember: the earlier you start this cataloguing process, the better. You should also keep on top of it so you don't have to spend hours cataloguing thousands of old images.

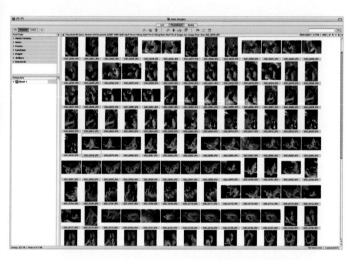

▶▶ Back-ups:

You should always burn a back-up CD or DVD of your work. Most computers now have a built-in CD burner, and some can also write to DVDs. CDs, which normally store 700MB of information, have come down in price over the last few years, and it is worth buying a decent brand to store your pictures. DVDs store a lot more information – around 4.75GB – and are therefore very useful for storing a lot of high-resolution

# GOING COMMERCIAL
## Can Your Movie Make Money?

As Hugh Hefner knows, there is money to be made from porn. Your best chance for success is to create a product for a mass market. What sells best is porn made by men, for men. It has been around for so long, and is being produced at such a high rate, that many people believe it is the only porn there is.

### Mass-Market Porn

There is a lot of porn around, and you really have to know what you are doing if you would like to compete on a commercial level. You need to find a studio and the necessary equipment, and get models and a crew at a good rate. If you decide to go down this route, here are some of the chief characteristics of mainstream porn:

▶▶ The film normally features aspiring or well-known porn stars. Female porn stars tend to have a sexual 'speciality'.

▶▶ The focus is on male fantasies and the pleasure of the male porn stars – come shots are a must. Man-on-man action is taboo.

▶▶ The scenes tend to be shot in the same studio, and not much thought is given to shooting, directing or editing creative scenarios that vary from the norm.

▶▶ An average 90-minute porn film tends to feature five to six sex scenes, which are sandwiched between badly acted, generally pointless non-sex scenes.

▶▶ Such films are produced on a relatively low budget, and make money by selling a few thousand copies through licensed websites and by mail order.

### Entering the Market

A good place to meet contacts in the industry is at any of the big erotic trade shows, such as the AVN in Las Vegas, the Venus Show in Berlin, and Erotica in London, where you will be able to meet many big porn producers.

▶▶ It makes sense to have a show reel with clips of erotic material you have created – hand them out along with your business card to producers that might be interested in publishing your material.

▶▶ If you have ideas for a future project, write a short proposal, and make sure you copyright it. Try to get a few minutes face-to-face with the person in charge of acquiring new projects, and take their business card.

---

 **PRACTICAL TIP: STAYING WITHIN THE LAW**

If would like to publish what you have created in your own bedroom, it is absolutely essential that you are familiar with the law. In most countries, for example, you need to have your film reviewed by a film classification authority. This is to make sure that the film does not contain 'indecent material' (although what this means varies from state to state and country to country). You will then have to pay to obtain a license, which will determine where and how you can sell your film. If you have any uncertainties about what you are doing, get some independent legal advice from a qualified practitioner – the penalties for breaking the law can be severe, so you really must act with caution.

---

▶▶ After the trade show, follow up your meetings with emails and at least one telephone call.

▶▶ If you are offering badly shot and unedited amateur footage, you might be wasting your time. Make sure whatever you hand out is at least shot and edited well. Better two minutes that are spot-on than 20 minutes that just don't work.

▶▶ Make sure your business card and anything else you hand out is also visually exciting and looks professional. The business card is particularly important, as it is generally the first impression someone gets of you. In my eyes, there is nothing worse than handing out a business card that you got printed one of those cheap machines for $5 half an hour before the meeting.

▶▶ If you think you have created something really exciting that you would like to share with the world, but don't have the budget to publish it yourself, you could always send it to a production company whose style you like. Bear in mind that unless they specialise in homemade porn, they may prefer to work with their well-known actors and experienced directors.

▶▶ Make sure that you have signed model-release forms from anybody featured in the film (see page 133 for more).

## Niche Markets

You might have artistic rather than commercial ambitions – some people try to get their work out there so that they can share their vision of erotica and inspire other people. It is an admirable thing to do, but you have to be prepared for the fact that you might lose money on your project.

Even if you shoot with amateur performers who do not expect to be paid, you still have to spend out on props and catering for everyone taking part and helping out. There is the cost of tape stock and other equipment, your time to shoot, log and edit the footage, and then the licensing for the film and music, the design of the cover, the duplication of the videos or DVDs, and possible advertising for your film.

All these costs add up, and if your film is creative and 'arty', chances are that although some people will absolutely love it, you won't sell the few thousand copies you need to recover your costs. You will cater to a niche market that will be delighted to have discovered your visual erotic gem, but you won't get rich.

## Online Options

A potentially cheaper option is to publish your video on the Web. In order to do this, it helps if you can design a website and know how to compress video for the Web (so that downloading will not take forever). You might need to pay a Web designer to do these jobs for you if you do not have all the necessary skills.

If you intend to charge for the downloads, be aware that most porn consumers get memberships from huge porn databanks for a month of unlimited downloads for as little as $19.99. They will expect more than just one video clip from your site if they have to pay to download your work. Most Internet-porn customers would expect regular updating and a big choice on a pay site.

## Keeping it Real

Ultimately, it all depends on your aims and expectations. Maybe you are perfectly happy to create sexy visuals for and with each other as one of many special experiences of your shared sensual journey. It will be exciting for the two of you to watch each other, and you can always choose to share your film with selected friends at a later date, rather than turning your intimate moments into a commercial venture.

# PROTECTING YOURSELF
## Safety and Privacy

If you shoot a pornographic video with your partner, you are taking a risk – even if both of you would never even dream of publishing the footage, it might still fall into the wrong hands. You can never guarantee your privacy, but the following chapter highlights potential pitfalls and explains some precautionary measures.

### Digital Images

Digital images, whether video, photographs or scanned prints, can be copied any number of times easily and without any loss of quality. They can also be stored in a variety of places – in the camera (or the camera's memory card), on CD or DVD, and on your computer's hard drive – making it hard to keep track of where they are. If you have a laptop, you might lose it or it might be stolen from your car. Your house might get burgled. These might seem like far-fetched scenarios, but it shows what could happen if you make more copies than are truly necessary.

Also, think about what might happen if you want to sell your computer on. You can back up all your data and reformat the hard drive so that it seems 'clean'; the problem is that even if you empty your recycle bin, you only allow the deleted files to be overwritten. If they have not been overwritten with new files yet, any old data can be restored relatively easy using various types of software.

If you are truly concerned about the possibility of your erotic images or videos falling into the wrong hands, make sure your originals and copies are kept in a safe, and try to at least 'hide' your sexy files on your hard drive – perhaps by requiring a password to access them, or not giving them obvious names. Do not sell any hard drives once you have stored erotic material on them, unless you have specialist 'shredding' software that actually destroys old files for good.

---

 **PRACTICAL TIP: BREAK-UPS**

Unfortunately, the biggest danger to your privacy can come form the person you least expect: your partner. If you break up with your partner, your relationship might turn sour and love might turn to hate. Hopefully this will never happen to you, but if it does and you happen to have created some erotic visuals together, it pays to have some form of a written agreement over the usage of those images.

You can write an agreement yourselves, in which case you should each keep a copy that both of you have signed. Alternatively, you can get legal advice on how best to word things – as long as you are not too embarrassed to tell your lawyer about your hobby! However, if you word your agreement clearly, and cover any eventuality you can think of, you should be safe. State that the pictures taken were for each other's enjoyment only, that the two of you are the joint copyright holders, and that the video is not intended for publication in any medium in any part of the world. You might want to add a clause stating that both of you will destroy the originals and any copies of the images you created together in the case of a break-up.

CD, and can use them in his/her modelling portfolio. Be careful what you offer in form of payment for publication of erotic images. The fact is that most artistic erotica magazines do not pay for the publication of your images, as they consider it to be free publicity for you and your work – in fact, some magazines even charge the photographer to publish their artwork!

Make sure whoever models for you is keen on having their pictures published and is aware of the long-term implications of agreeing to sign a release form. There is no way back if they suddenly get together with a new and possibly possessive partner, or if they take a job (such as school teaching) in which the unearthing of erotic images could cause a major problem.

## Model-Release Forms

If you do intend to publish any of the pictures you have shot of a lover, partner or friend, make sure that they have signed a model-release form and that you have seen ID confirming that they are over 18 years old.

In the release form, the filmmaker/photographer needs to state precisely where they intend to use the videos or stills (even if you would like unlimited usage in any medium worldwide, you need to state this). You also give a time frame for this usage (again, even if this is unlimited). The model needs to state whether he or she is expecting any payment in the event of publication, and what percentage is split between photographer and model in the event that the publication makes a profit. Many photographers do not pay their models when they start out but offer a TFP (Time For Print) deal, where the model poses in exchange for copies of the images taken. He or she will receive these as prints or on a

---

**▶▶| PRACTICAL TIP: ESSENTIAL PROTECTION**

The importance of release forms cannot be underestimated. Always, always make sure your models or performers sign them (ideally before the session, so that if the model suddenly changes his or her mind you haven't wasted your time and effort on a shoot that can't be used). Even if you know someone very well and trust him or her implicitly, do not just accept their word – make sure they sign a release from. If you don't have a release form, you have no proof that the model/performer agreed to the use/publication of their intimate images. If you publish these pictures without their written consent and they are unhappy about it, they may well be able to sue you.

# 7 ▶▶ REFERENCES AND RES

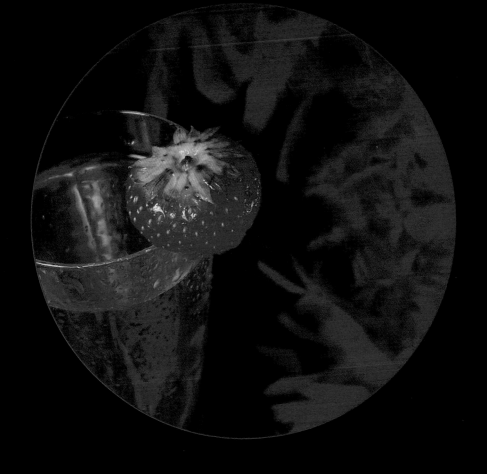

RCES

# TEN TOP TIPS
## Advice from the Naked Pornographer

❶ Forget everything you know about glamour models and porn stars. See your partner and yourself with fresh eyes. Realise what makes each of you sexy and unique, and capture this essence on film.

❷ Enjoy the ride! Do not compromise an orgasm for a potentially hot shot. Unless you are a porn pro who is paid to act and only has an orgasm if they are lucky, you are here to have fun!

❸ Don't get drunk. You might feel like a sex god or goddess, but you won't be. It'll make painful viewing – assuming that you've managed to get anything in focus.

❹ Have a good concealer handy for pimples and rashes.

❺ Use ice cubes for pert nipples.

❻ Have loads of good-quality silk-based lube handy to give body parts and toys that extra shine. Avoid oil-based lube: it's an overdone 80s-glamour prop, sticks rather than slides, stains sheets and destroys condoms.

❼ Encourage your partner to do what they enjoy doing rather than trying to turn them into a professional porn star. 'Deep throat' or 'double penetration' is not everyone's idea of fun.

❽ Direct your model(s) and performer(s). Never assume who is posing for you knows what to do. It is not enough to just 'point and shoot' if you want to create stylish and sexy images that are more than just your average 'readers' wives' shots.

❾ Don't get too hung up about hard-ons. If you enjoy yourself and each other and forget about the camera, a hard-on will come eventually. In the meantime, do other things that you enjoy like kissing, stroking and oral sex.

❿ The 'money shot' is not obligatory. The whole idea about great sex is that you loose control and just enjoy yourself, rather than time your orgasm for the camera. Guys – don't sacrifice her orgasm for a cum shot!

# GLOSSARY
## Some Useful Terms

**Aperture**

The opening that controls the amount of light entering through the lens

**Ambient sound**

The general background sound that is audible on the set (not including dialogue)

**Available light**

A general term for the light (natural or artificial) available on a location before intervention of the filmmaker

**CCD (Charge Coupled Device)**

The 'film' of digital cameras. It turns light into an electronic signal

**Cutaway**

A shot that will enable you to edit a sequence. It could show a detail of an action that has also been recorded in a wide shot. For example, if a wide shot shows two people kissing, the cutaway could be a close-up of their locked lips

**Depth of field**

The area of apparent sharpness in an image. A wide-angle lens gives a greater depth of field than a telephoto lens

**Diffuser**

Translucent white material or a 'softbox' that is attached in front of a lamp or flash to soften the light quality and reduce its intensity and harshness

**Digital zoom**

A camera feature that gives the illusion of a telephoto lens by enlarging a part of the image. Because it simply crops and then enlarges a portion of the frame, the image actually suffers from quality loss

***Dissolve***

A soft transition during editing. One shot fades out while the other one fades in

**Drop-out**

The reduction of quality – especially in visuals – that occurs as analogue footage is copied. Manifests itself in a white line that runs through the image

**Exposure compensation**

A function of many cameras that allows you to override autoexposure settings (by decreasing or increasing the exposure in increments) through the push of a button

**Gel**

Coloured transparent foils that can be placed over tungsten lights or windows to change the colour of light

**Key light**

The main light in a three-point lighting system. The exposure is set to match this light

**Linear editing**

Chronological film editing performed by copying footage from tape to tape.

**JPEG**

A standard file format used to store digital photographs. The compression to this format is 'lossy', which means that it entails a loss in quality compared to non-compression formats like TIFFs

**Noise**

An unwanted image degradation that can appear in digital images

**Non-linear editing**

A digital editing system that is flexible at all times and allows quick changes in the order or duration of shots

**Optical viewfinder**

*A viewfinder system that shows what the lens 'sees'. Standard in SLR cameras*

**Pan**

*A horizontal camera move performed with the camera either on the tripod or handheld*

**Pixel (Picture element)**

*The tiniest element that digital pictures are made of.*

**PPI (Pixels/Points Per Inch)**

*A measure of the resolution of digital printers, scanners and images. 300ppi is a good standard for printed digital images*

**Set**

*The location where you shoot stills or a film. It is usually altered to the specifications of the photographer or filmmaker*

**Shutter speed**

*The duration for which the film or image sensor is exposed to light. A slow shutter speed allows for creatively blurred photos or video scenes*

**Telephoto lens**

*A lens that makes things look closer than they are in reality (like binoculars)*

**Thumbnail**

*A small, stamp-like version of an image. Thumbnails allow easy browsing through image folders as they can be viewed in batches rather than opening each image individually*

**Time code**

*Numeric recording on a tape that can be displayed on the LCD screen or in the viewfinder and gives a reference for locating specific shots. Very handy for editing*

**Tungsten lamp**

*A specific type of artificial light. This could be a light with a domestic bulb or a powerful 'redhead' film light*

**White balance**

*A facility in digital cameras that enables the accurate recording of the colour temperature of light. Manual options are handy to override the auto settings in difficult light situations such as sunsets. The manual settings also give the photographer a choice of making*

*the images look blue or reddish in tone, independently from what the actual light on the set is*

**Wild track**

*Recorded ambient sound from the location. Useful in the edit to fill possible gaps in usable sound*

**Wide-angle lens**

*A lens with a wide field of view. Particularly useful in small spaces*

**Zoom lens**

*A lens with an adjustable focal length. Some can range from wide-angle to telephoto*

**Zoom in**

*Makes a subject seem bigger in the frame and closer to the lens*

**Zoom out**

*Makes a subject seem smaller and further away*

# BIBLIOGRAPHY AND VIDEOGRAPHY
## Some Recommended Viewing

## RECOMMENDED FILMS

### Behind the Green Door
*Directed by the Mitchell Brothers. 1972, 72 min*

*A classic porn film. Famous for its trapeze and orgy scenes that shine courtesy of a creative choice of setting, props and acting.*

### Love's Passion
*Veronica Hart. 1998*

*This has become a female-directed porn classic. The big romantic storyline and period costume acting is not to everyone's taste, but the sex scenes are gripping. Hart focuses on real female orgasms rather than the usual male cum shots. The artistic camerawork is inspirational.*

### Orgasm: Faces of Ecstacy
*Joani Blank/Marianna Beck/Jack Hafferkamp. 2004, 55 min*

*A tribute to the power and beauty of orgasm that is shown on the faces of 22 participants. Rather than showing disembodied body parts during sex, the camera focuses on the faces of those experiencing ecstasy. Refreshingly intimate.*

### The Fashonistas
*Directed by John (Buttman) Stagliano. 2002, 280 min*

*An award-winning fetish film that has become a cult classic. The whips and chains are not everyone's preference and some women might find this film offensive. However, this is a prime example of the successful use of creative props, skillful camerawork and lighting, and clever editing.*

### Whipsmart
*A Good Vibrations/Sexpositive Productions video. 2001, 82 min*

*A good introduction to S&M play. The presenter and dominatrix, Mistress Morgana, guides viewers through communication, spanking, role-play and bondage. Creative scenes such as S&M play on a kitchen table convey a great sense of humour.*

## RECOMMENDED WEBSITES

### www.goodvibes.com
*A great online resource for erotic books, toys and films. Lots of information and female-friendly artwork. Also information on all sorts of erotic workshops.*

### www.nerve.com
*A fantastic site featuring erotic photography and writing. All contemporary, fresh and new. Guaranteed 'sleaze-free' zone.*

### www.shootingpeople.org
*A fantastic site with low membership fees for aspiring filmmakers. It delivers daily bulletins about training, jobs and equipment, and helps members to network by allowing them to post and exchange enquiries and tips.*

# RECOMMENDED BOOKS

### Babylon Blue: Illustrated History of Erotic Cinema
*David Flint, 1998*

*The book examines the 1960s roots of modern-day erotic cinema – from naturist films to Russ Meyer. Featuring profiles of key directors, producers and performers, and detailed critiques of the finest adult movies of all time.*

### Get the Most from Your Digital Camera
*Simon Joinson, 2004*

*A very visual book teaching technical and creative aspects of digital photography in general.*

### Nerve: The New Nude
*Edited by Genevieve Field, 2000*

*A 'coffee-table' book of contemporary erotic photography. Young, fresh and exciting – purely visual.*

### Photo Sex: Fine Art Sexual Photography Comes of Age
*Edited by David Steinberg, 2003*

*Explicit and erotic fine-art photography that ventures past the clichés of glamour and porn. It shows people of all ages and sexual orientations in sexual ecstasy.*

### Photography for Perverts
*Charles Gatewood, 2003*

*A very practical book full of great tips for the aspiring erotic photographer. Focuses on the fetish scene.*

### Annie Sprinkle: Post-Porn Modernist
*Annie Sprinkle, 1998*

*An inspirational book of this fearless and creative erotic artist. Lots of food for thought regarding crossing over boundaries to achieve sexual liberation.*

### The Mammoth Book of Erotic Photography
*Edited by Maxim Jakubowski and Marylin Jayne Lewis, 2001*

*A striking selection of erotic black-and-white photography. Affordable and inspirational.*

### The Ultimate Guide to Adult Videos: How to Watch Adult Videos and Make Your Sex Life Sizzle
*Violet Blue, 2003*

*A great library book to have. 300-plus candid reviews of adult films. Includes a glossary of porn terms.*

# INDEX

# CREDITS
## Petra Joy

I would like to dedicate this book to all my models – for feeling rather than faking it!


Thanks to:


Dom for glowing with spirituality and sensuality.

Emma C. for putting her hard-earned cash where her mouth was.

Gillian for showing the world how sexy a 46-year-old mother of two can be by being herself.

Hellen and Jonathan (www.flamingfun.com) for being such a gorgeous couple and great performance artists.

Jen (www.jentheroo.com) for being a gorgeous, patient and professional model and performance artist.

James from Quid Publishing for his creative co-operation.

Lee Anne for being sexy in a pink dress.

Paul (www.harrisondesign.com) for his amazing light objects, props and sets.


Special Thanks to:


Emilia Ren and Slim Da Silva for being my first-ever nude models, and trusting, inspiring
and supporting me when I most needed it.

And Tony for many late, late nights in front of a computer,
and for discovering the many Tex spots.